Corporate Soul

by Jaffer Ali

Very special thanks to...

This might be the most difficult part of writing *Corporate Soul* because the book represents so many people teaching me along the journey. But without a doubt, everything that I am or hope to ever be is based upon the love and wisdom that my father demonstrated when he was alive. He has been dead for almost 20 years and yet his spirit is with me always. No tribute is adequate to explain how many ways this wonderful man touched my heart.

There are others who have made a significant contribution to the journey that led to this book. Waleed and Malik Ali, my uncles, provided nurturing when I needed it most. My partners at Fusion, Rod Bothwell and Tom Matthews, guys I also grew up with, helped me understand how working together made a difference. But my sister/partner Anisa Ali and cousin/partner Tom Zegar are colleagues that are unbelievable sources of inspiration. Working with them is not work but an unfolding of the true spiritual path.

I also happen to be married to a woman who has taught me more about Soul than anybody. My wife Carol has turned a workaholic into someone who appreciates a beautiful sunset, a squirrel running up a tree, and the generosity of a warm smile. She has made our home an oasis.

Last but not least are the two ladies who have managed to turn my grammatical pig Latin into intelligible prose. They would be the team of Gail Rimkus and Allison Martin. Whatever is readable is in large measure due to them. I hope you all have half as much fun reading this as I have had writing it.

* * * Table of Contents * * *

Preface

"The heart of a fool is in his mouth, but the mouth of a wise man is in his heart."
  --Benjamin Franklin

"The greatest discovery of my generation is that human beings can alter their lives by altering their attitudes of mind."
  --William James

There is no simple way to speak about Soul. When we combine its discussion in relation to corporate institutions, then this presents even more difficulty. Nothing worthwhile is easy and the following discussion borrows from a wide spectrum of disciplines from physics, psychology, ecology, and philosophy. The reader is encouraged to treat each chapter as an exercise in discovery. While all of the individual chapters are connected to each other in a general, common theme, an attempt was made to have each stand on its own. They are almost a collection of essays with the hope that by the end of the book an understanding of Corporate Soul shall emerge.

We talk around the subject and speak about the Soul's myriad reflections rather than its direct reality. This is because we cannot touch it, measure it, see it, etc., except through indirect means. This is uncomfortable at first because our language limits us in revealing the nature and workings of Soul. Limits come from trying to apply a language borrowed from science. The Jungian analyst, June Singer wrote in *Boundaries of the Soul*:

> "The word 'science' comes from the Latin scientia, which means knowledge, and therefore is identified with the intellectual effort to draw into consciousness as much knowledge as possible. [It] is necessary to recognize that there is a very large area of human experience with which science cannot deal. It has to do with all that is neither finite nor measurable, with all that is neither distinct nor explicable. It is that which is not accessible to logic. It begins at the outermost edge of knowledge. Despite the continuing expansion or even explosion of information, there will forever be limits beyond which the devices of science cannot lead a man."

The following chapters do not deal with the science of business. They deal with the art of business and must of necessity deal with Soul, for the source of all art rests in the realm of experience beyond the finite, measurable world of reason, logic and science.

But why Corporate Soul? The answers are simple. Business can and should be a sacred enterprise. Corporations can be an agent for transforming society if Soul can lead us to a new vision of reality. Whether we are CEOs, managers or line employees, we all spend so much of our time at work. The idea that business can be sacred or spiritual makes all of that time we spend take on a whole new meaning.

The following chapters are about trying to penetrate this meaning. As the new millennium draws on, we see a hungering for a more spiritual existence coming forward. Ethics are once again a major topic of discussion in all of our major intellectual pursuits. The problems of integrating the mind, body, and spirit in our everyday lives is the milieu for undertaking a book about Corporate Soul.

It is with the utmost humility that this author hopes the reader will determine your own meaning of Soul and discover the possibilities of creating a new vision of reality. A soulful vision allows us to transform corporate institutions, and eventually society, in preparation of a bold new future.

The New 2001 Introduction...

This book was written almost five years ago before embarking on creating a new company. Reflecting on the last five years is an overwhelming experience. Implementing the tenets of Corporate Soul has been one of the most spiritual times of my life. Actually, this is an ongoing spiritual experience. Writing *Corporate Soul* in 1996 and then trying to live up to the ideals has been gratifying. This prologue is a brief history of the journey. Along the way there will be references to chapters in the book that give meaning to the journey.

Before selling my interests in a fulfillment and catalog company in 1996, I had grown increasingly interested in the spiritual nature of man. This often happens when one becomes acutely aware that the sand in one's hourglass is emptying with inexorable speed. If one is lucky you become aware that too often business and the concept of "soul" are compartmentalized, each tucked in its own little corner. This awareness overwhelmed me. Selling my interests in the business I had helped to create was difficult, but necessary if I was going to start the journey. That is also when *Corporate Soul* began to take shape as a book.

Together with my sister and cousin, who had also explored their spirituality, we decided to embark on creating a company that placed spirituality at the forefront of our corporate vision. Together (and "together" is the operative word), we began our journey of creating an entity that would satisfy both our economic and spiritual needs. It was not always easy. In fact, we nearly went broke. Ross Perot once remarked that most entrepreneurs are too passionate to consider going out of business, and this passion is what saves them. Make sure you pay special attention to the chapter on passion.

In 1996 we were marketing videos via television direct response. At the end of the year we secured the television direct response rights to an Irish performance video called "Riverdance." Unexpectedly, this became the hit of the year for 1997. In fact, we won an award for best commercial of the year. But as time passed, we tried to match its success with follow-up campaigns for other videos. Rising television media rates caused a string of financial debacles...20 campaigns in a row to be exact. We closed the year hanging on by a thread.

Then at the beginning of 1998 everyone in our small company got AOL accounts. Going online proved to be just the right thing at the right time. We began to connect with all kinds of people in a dizzying example of synchronicity. It seemed like day after day, information that would eventually lead to the success of our enterprise seemed to "pop" up out of nowhere. This is almost a textbook definition of synchronicity (see the chapter so titled). Following our instincts, in May of 1998 we transformed our company into an "Internet" company.

We sold videos online. This was a bold step, since none of us even knew how to use online search engines, let alone understand how the Internet worked. We did everything we could on the cheap. The decisions we made were not so much analytical as they were intuitive. We jumped in, even though we did not know the industry language, did not know the industry players, did not know much of anything relating to the Internet at all. The chapter titled "Intuition" explores the role it plays in creating a solid business.

We named our company "Pulse" and had a catchy corporate tag line, "Listening and Responding to the Rhythms of the World." Catchy phrasing aside, futility was our initial reward. We tried to sell South Park videos inside highly targeted sites. We actually found over 1100 different websites that were exclusively on South Park. Results? Miserable...but we never despaired since we viewed each "failure" as a learning experience. We tried selling military videos inside history and military oriented web sites. Results? More learning...

We took "streaming" video clips and tried to sell videos this way. Results? More learning...We created audio banners to sell videos like "A Hard Day's Night" and "The Bee Gees." We tried every conceivable marketing method on the Internet possible. The operative term in all of this is the word "tried" because back then we did a lot more trying than we did selling.

As is often the case in life, what appeared bad for us was actually a blessing in disguise. For six months, we had nearly set a record for marketing futility. But along the way, this futility taught us all about every kind of marketing method on the Internet. In six months, we had become close to experts on marketing, and we began to share this knowledge in articles and online discussion groups. The Internet promised to be a new environment where information was shared...and we shared it with all that would listen.

But there was a large problem looming. We were going broke. We had not taken a paycheck for an entire year. In fact, we all had taken second mortgages on our homes to pay the non-family workers their salaries. Also, our futility was costing a great deal of money. The marketing education we were receiving came at a price.

I remember feeling that we were being tested. I mean, here we were, broke, borrowing on our homes, and we had absolutely no answer to our business dilemma. If this did not test our "Corporate Soul" it is hard to imagine what would. To complicate matters slightly, my partner/cousin just had his first child. In short, it felt that our soulful journey was running out of road.

For some reason, we continued on. Looking back, it could only have been an act of faith to keep trying new marketing ideas online. It certainly was not some master business plan that we were implementing. We had NO IDEA where we were headed except the poor house. Just as we were at our wits' end, something that to this day seemed like a miracle happened. Someone had sent a daily joke publication to me (I cannot even remember who forwarded it to me). I distinctly remember that the joke was funny. At the bottom of the email publication was an email address to request advertising information.

I sent an email and to my delight, within 60 seconds, got an auto-responder with all of the details. Tom, my cousin and partner, called the proprietor of the publication and he took our credit card information over the phone to place our first ad inside an email publication. Within 24 hours of finding this new advertising medium, our 50-word text ad (selling the European version of "Candid Camera" on video) was running inside "Joke A Day." Within 48 hours the orders for the video poured in! In fact, we made a 500% return on our ad investment with that single ad.

This sounds too much like a Hollywood script. But it is true nonetheless. We figured that if this ad worked in one humor email publication, why not try a few more? Within three weeks, we had found a marketing solution and began advertising regularly inside 16 online publications…all of them delivered via email to their subscriber base. The total number of subscribers each ad would hit was slightly over 600,000. We decided to purchase one of the humor publications. It was named "The Daily Joke" and had 74,000 subscribers. We purchased it for only $7400.

Once again, we were following our intuition because now we were entering into the online publishing business, and we had no idea how this worked. Yet we continued onward, almost oblivious to the challenges ahead.

We renamed the publication "Laff A Day." We figured that we could cut down our ad costs and sell twice as many videos inside the publication since it contained two ads per issue. Then, sometime in November, we decided that maybe we could sell one of the ads to outside marketers and keep one of the ads for internal marketing.

The main stumbling block, so we thought, was that none of us had ever sold advertising. We certainly had purchased enough of it over the years, but selling ads was not something in our experience. We thought the solution was to contact all of the major online media companies and ask them if they would like to sell 74,000 ad impressions a day for us. This amounted to over 2 million ad impressions for them to sell a month. We also knew from all of our marketing that this medium actually worked. It was not a theoretical idea. We had advertised with all of the online media companies, tried every kind of online marketing, and the ONLY marketing avenue that generated profits was advertising inside these publications that were delivered via email…and in a text format only.

Then came THE DATE, as we call it around here. As has been the case time and time again, what we had thought was bad for us turned out to be good. Miraculously, none of the online media companies were interested in representing our advertising inventory. Not a single one of them even cared when we told them that this advertising medium really worked. We shared with them the numbers of several past ad campaigns, contrasting that with banner campaign results. The lack of interest was one of the most bewildering things in my life, and one of the most thankful business accidents as well.

THE DATE was November 30, 1998 and I had just gotten off the phone with the last online media network. This major online media company told me that they had no interest in representing any of our advertising inventory. After hanging up, quite exasperated, I got my sister and cousin together and said, "If nobody wants to sell our advertising inventory, why don't we get all of the email publications we are advertising in and create a network of publications delivered via email?" To my delight, they both said, "Why not?"

I wrote a one-page contract for the publications to sign that said we would find advertisers for them. They liked us already since we had been paying them money every week and buying advertising that featured different videos. All of the 15 outside newsletter publications (each of the publishers called their publications "newsletters") signed the document. On November 30, 1998, The Pulse Email Newsletter Network (PENN) was born along with a new corporate name: Penn Media.

As any parent knows, bringing a baby into this world is less work than nurturing him/her. In our own version of "Field of

Dreams," we had built a network but we had no idea if advertisers would come. Once again, we were touched by blessings. Earlier I told you about how we had participated in online discussion groups. One was run by an online media agent by the name of John Audette. He was a bright man with what I call an "informed heart." We gravitated toward each other, probably sensing a connection. When we created PENN, I called him up and told him pretty much the same story outlined here. Instead of indifference, he suggested I speak to his online media guy.

Within 10 days, they placed an ad for one of their clients. The client was this little company called "INTEL." The ad ran to 610,000 subscribers inside the PENN network on December 10, 1998. One week later, we sold another ad to someone who had read an article I wrote. Within 17 days, we had sold two ads to the entire network. Sure, it was before Christmas. Sure, it was in the boom days of the Internet. Sure, we were lucky beyond having any right to expect.

We were still broke and not taking a salary. We wanted to own a few more publications, and so we purchased some and decided to create others. We purchased "The Daily Recipe" and created three other publications. The last week in December, I wrote the business plan while my cousin diligently continued to recruit new newsletters to the network. My sister was (and still is) in charge of our owned and operated content as well as video marketing.

The rest is history. Today, as I write this in May of 2001, PENN Media is the largest privately held publishing and media company on the Internet. We have over 1000 email publications in the network that include over 60 million opt in subscribers under contract. We now own 77 of the publications while contracting with the others to represent their advertising space.

We remained true to our values and in the process created an environment filled with Corporate Soul. This could not have happened if we did not take the principles in the pages that follow seriously.

Jaffer Ali
May 2001

Introduction

"If you sense that a profound change is happening in the business world, but you're not quite sure what it is; if you've noticed that old visions and strategies don't seem to work anymore; if you need to learn new ways to lead, you are not alone. Throughout the world, people in business--including owners, managers, and employees--are changing the way they work. They are engaged in a transformation that some have said is as great as any in history. This shift is leading to the new paradigm in business."

--Michael Ray from, *What Is The New Paradigm In Business*

When the idea first came to me about writing a business book dealing with Soul, many business associates thought I had grown a bit "touched." Why would anyone fresh from Harvard with an MBA or any hard-nosed business man read a treatise about developing Soul as a corporate objective?

The answer is rather simple. There is an emerging awareness that what is necessary in today's business environment as well as the world is the caring of Soul. Corporations, large and small, need to develop Soul in order to thrive and prepare for the next century and beyond.

If necessity is the "Mother of Invention," then it just may be the case that necessity is also a parent to soulful business as well. The present environment demands a new way to confront the challenges. In the Eighties we had the S&L scandals that brought the greed and corruption to a head. Today we find ourselves in the midst of increased competition. Corporate excess has led to overregulated industries, and we are now in the midst of severe downsizing of our industrial giants. We find ourselves in a world with exploding choices and an information glut outpacing our ability to comprehend.

Today's generation of workers and executives work longer and harder than a generation ago, yet this seems not enough. We suffer from a nation of addicts. Alcohol and other drugs not only numb our work force but our corporate boardrooms as well. It is folly to believe that the ills of society at large are not also the ills of our corporate culture.

A major premise of this book is that all of our institutions reflect and mutually reinforce the prevailing philosophical and scientific attitudes of their time. This is true with educational, religious and, of course, corporate institutions. This will be explored in more detail in the chapter, "The New Paradigm." Not only is it the case that our institutions reflect our attitudes, they in some way reflect, as if in a mirror, our Soul.

So what do we mean by Soul? We all have a rudimentary understanding of this word. But as soon as we try to define it, we get hopelessly bogged down in metaphysical language. This is neither fun to read nor write. Our approach to what Soul is will be rather to look at its reflected qualities. Passion, responsibility, leadership, and humanity will be examined throughout this book. Each chapter in most ways stands on its own. By talking around the subject, it is hoped that by the end of the book the reader will have an understanding of what developing Corporate Soul means, but probably will be no closer to a strict definition.

In any case, your own view of Soul will suffice. We instinctively attribute good things to Soul. Soul food or Soul music usually speaks to something that is good for us on a fundamental level, something deep inside us. This kind of understanding will help in understanding the nature of this book.

If Corporate Soul is to mean anything at all, we have to look at what corporations are and what they have become. One of the first lessons one learns when incorporating is that a corporation is like a person. In fact the word "corporation" comes from the root word "corpus" which means "body." This body assumes rights and is considered a legal entity. In the eyes of the law, the corporation can sue, be sued, is taxed and can even die. So why not endow this body with Soul?

The concept of Soul also implies something greater than ourselves. It connects us to the infinite. Tapping into this source can be a liberating experience and frees us from total reliance on reason and an oppressive information flow. To treasure reason, rationality, knowledge, or information above all other considerations does not lead to the Promised Land of success. Patton's eloquent essay, "The Secret of Victory," in chapter 10 speaks to the limits of this thinking.

Everybody is generally aware of the information explosion. It is estimated that the total amount of information in the world is doubling now at the rate of every three years. This has further caused information to become compartmentalized and created more and more specialists in every field from medicine to, not surprisingly, business.

But information alone cannot cure the ills of society any more than it can solve business problems. If you own your own business, you need more than information. You need to find a way to connect the network of pieces of information. You must discover how to integrate this information into a cohesive whole.

Finding the interconnection of seemingly disparate pieces of information is about developing Soul. Making decisions under the tremendous burden of uncertainty is about developing Soul. Uncertainty is only a burden insofar as we perceive it to be. In the East, the symbol for "crisis" also means "opportunity." It depends upon how we view the reality. Working out new relationships within an organization beyond standard hierarchical relationships is about developing Soul.

And, of course, introducing values based upon the notion that we are connected to each other as if we are cells in a body is about developing Soul.

Introducing Soul into one's business is not about religion, although it may be a spiritual quest. It has much to do with appreciating the wonder, mystery and power of unfolding events. One very successful entrepreneur, Lillian Vernon, the mail order magnate, once said that she had never experienced an unsuccessful test mailing or product. To be sure there were many tests that lost considerable money, but how were these deemed successful?

It is no Orwellian twist in logic to have a successful test even though one had miserable results. Ms. Vernon fully grasped that the lessons learned from each transaction have more importance to the total business experience than the profit or loss gained from that particular transaction. She developed a different calculus of success than reducing the notion of success to each transaction. This new calculus is about corporate Soul.

Another key component of corporate Soul is the introduction of real responsibility to the business environment. It is not surprising that this has been absent from corporate thinking for so many years. Responsibility has been absent in almost every phase of modern society from science, family, and education to even medicine. We have devoted an entire chapter to the various levels of responsibility in the corporate environment.

It is a startling phenomenon that the elimination of human values from the calculus of decision-making at every level of society has been elevated to the ideal. Values have been relegated to religious groups who coincidentally have given only lip service to the concept. For validation of this lip service, one need only examine that more people have been killed in the name of religion than any other single principle in the history of mankind. Soul has even been torn away from religion.

It makes no difference how large or small your business is, to develop Corporate Soul and a healthy organization requires you to think about how relationships are to be worked out within your organization. One needs to ask questions about right and wrong. What is the right way to interact with your suppliers? If they double ship you a load of widgets without invoicing you twice, do you thank fortune for smiling upon you? Do you contact them and either return the product or ask to be billed?

How are you going to interact with your customers or clients? I have been working in the direct marketing industry for several years, and it was not hard to see which companies had developed Soul versus those that had not. There are many industry clichés that illustrate the negative side of the ledger.

Have you ever heard that "Product is King?" This means that the product is the most important part of the promotion, not the customer. A prominent in-bound telemarketing company was fond of telling their clients that "...our motto is we believe in mass not class." This marked a philosophy and value system that dictated that they could answer many calls but eliminated the possibility of doing a great job. A great job was not even part of their objective!

Another illustration of ethical problems in the industry was a media buyer telling a client of ours, "...You have to understand that the consumer has the intelligence of a retarded chimpanzee, and you have to communicate with them on this level." This was not meant to be funny but sincere advice for running a successful promotion. Obviously thinking and then treating one's customers as chimpanzees is not marketing with Soul. We have much to say about this in the marketing chapter.

Issues concerning corporate values pop up all the time. How you deal with these, in part, determines what kind of company you have. They define your corporate character. There is a balance sheet item called "Goodwill." Banks rarely understand it. They rarely have Soul. It is considered an "intangible asset." But what is this asset? I think it has a great deal to do with corporation's Soul. Because this is exceedingly difficult to quantify, it is not spoken about very often in business schools across the country. When I was studying business at the University of Illinois, the operative principle was that if you could not count it, it did not exist. Corporate Soul does not surrender to quantification.

As a business executive making decisions affecting the lives of not just your family but the lives of people who work for you and their families, it is often an overwhelming responsibility. Developing a keen awareness of this responsibility is also about developing Soul. Responsibilities are like a series of concentric circles that need not conflict. The collapse of responsibility and its essential necessity to corporate affairs is detailed in Chapter 6.

One of the least understood and mysterious phenomenon is the connection between one's internal, "personal" dramas and external events. It is almost as if our psyche is a mirror that reflects these external events and a window allowing us to see through our experiences. Have you ever been in personal turmoil and observed simultaneously how your business also reflected this turmoil? Often this personal anxiety is the necessary component in solving a marketing dilemma or operational problem. We have been taught to ignore echoes of our inner experiences. This thesis is explored in more detail in the speculative "Synchronicity" chapter.

It has been thought in the past that inner experiences are for poets and artists, not businesspeople. Some believe looking inside one's self for answers to problems leads to selfish indulgence. The true search for Soul is selfless, and developing corporate Soul requires a journey into exploring the realm of inner experiences. What keeps this journey from being mystical and self indulgent is its concrete application to the world at large. What is intuition? Has it a place in corporate America? We will attempt to answer this as well.

We will explain what we mean about introducing passion and energy into the corporate environment. It is certainly hoped that after reading *Corporate Soul* you are left with the idea that there is so much more to developing our corporate institutions than what we were taught in business school. We need to view our enterprise with a reverence that is all too often missing with our top executives. We must move beyond viewing our existence in "Zero-Sum Game" (Chapter 2) terms.

This book is an attempt to introduce concepts from a wide area of thought and hopefully make them meaningful to the corporate executive. We all have the power to learn a new way. The great philosopher Plato said:

> "The Soul of every man does possess the power to learn the truth...Just as one must have to turn the body round in order that the eyes should see the light instead of darkness, so Soul must be turned away from this changing world until its eye can begin to contemplate reality."

By allowing Soul to enter into our business environment, our corporations become a powerful vehicle for transforming society. There is no easy and quick-fix way to discover and apply Soul to one's personal or professional life. There is no single path for every one of us to follow. This is the exciting part about the journey of discovery. We each must choose our own paths, and whether you choose the one less traveled or one well worn, the journey is what truly makes all the difference.

Chapter One

The New Paradigm

"We have come to accept materialism dogmatically, despite its failure to account for the most familiar experience of our daily lives. In short, we have an inconsistent world-view. Our predicament has fueled the demand for a new paradigm--a unifying world-view that will integrate mind and spirit into science."

--A. Goswami, *The Self-Aware Universe*

There is a school of scientific and philosophical thought called "Cartesian Rationalism." A major tenet of this is that everything can be reduced to the material world. Matter is everything, and if one had enough information, one could determine the future. One would need to know the position and velocity of all the matter in the universe and then one could conceptually predict everything forever. This idea was best summarized in 1819, by French physicist, Pierre Laplace:

> "Consider an intelligence, which at any instant, could have knowledge of all forces controlling nature together with the momentary conditions of all the entities of which nature consists. If this intelligence were powerful enough to submit all this data to analysis, it would be able to embrace in a single formula the movements of the largest bodies in the universe and those of the lightest atoms; for nothing would be uncertain; the future and the past would be present to its eyes."

This school of materialistic thought led mankind from the grip of superstition. Things happened in predictable ways, not by random chance caused by mythological gods or magic. This led to the creation of the scientific method which allowed us to increase our knowledge of the physical world. This was a major paradigm shift which today still holds many within its grip.

Cartesian Rationalism also fits nicely with the science of its time. In fact, in many ways the classical mechanics or physics of Isaac Newton owes much to Rene Descartes. In this new emerging world-view (or cosmological view), the universe and everything in it were thought to be mechanistic. Even human beings were thought to be machines.

Within this framework, if one needed to understand anything better, one only needed to reduce the problem down to smaller and smaller components. Reduction to finer and finer degrees became the way reality was viewed. Information and knowledge itself became compartmentalized as the paradigm developed. The materialistic, mechanistic view of the universe left little room for Soul. And the split occurred in which Soul became the sole province of religion. Prior to this split, Soul was a legitimate topic of interest in every aspect of reality including art, science, and especially work. In the midst of all this, the modern corporation was born.

In every aspect of human endeavor, this paradigm created the framework for our perception of the world. We create our reality by the way we think. The corporation was born in an atmosphere that treated humans as machines. So it is not surprising that the workplace reflected this reality. Obviously machines have no feelings and if Man was just another type of machine, he had no feelings either. The mass production lines along with steel and coal mines of the 20th century captured the essence of a philosophy where laborers were thought to be no better than pieces of equipment.

Everyone has a philosophical orientation whether we are conscious of it or not. This orientation or framework acts as a filter for our perception of reality. Our conscious and unconscious worlds are shaped by this framework. In turn, we tend to create institutions that reflect this paradigm. If we think of the universe in materialistic, mechanistic terms, then this filter pervades our consciousness and has concrete consequences. It is not just our corporations that reflect this paradigm. Our political system, educational institutions, religious institutions and even families often reflect this philosophical orientation.

But this paradigm also creates a framework for solving many problems. Armed with the scientific method and reason, we could predict and hypothesize. We were freed from mystical causes. Even the nature and scope of how we solve ordinary problems have had a mechanistic methodology. The corporate executive or manager confronted with a problem may choose to sit down with a blank piece of paper and begin to write down the pros and cons of each course of action. It is as if one could choose the proper course with the most points on the side of the ledger. A cousin to this is the old cost/benefit analysis taught by every business school.

An illustration of this methodology can be recalled from our grade school teachings of Ben Franklin. Remember what good old Ben did when he wanted to become the perfect human being? He got out a pad of paper and wrote down all the qualities he thought of as good and those he thought of as bad. He then had a well-reasoned road map to perfection. All he had to do was work on eliminating the negative qualities and work on keeping the good qualities. Ralph Kramden of "The Honeymooners" (with Ed Norton's help) tried to do the same thing! Even a Bing Crosby tune captured the essence of this paradigm, "...You have to accentuate the positive, eliminate the negative, latch on to the affirmative and don't mess with Mr. Inbetween."

If nothing else, we should see how a world-view penetrates our culture. The journey from Rene Descartes to Ben Franklin, Ralph Kramden and a Bing Crosby melody is only the proverbial tip of the iceberg. The Cartesian paradigm and Newtonian mechanics have not only carried us a long way but continue to be the dominant orientation for solving problems and viewing reality. It is also the case that our multi-billion dollar corporations owe their existence to this world-view.

In a mechanistic universe there is no room for Soul. Newton did not want his major work published until after his death because he grasped this quite well and did not want to war with the clergy any more than he had already done. If everything in the universe, including Man, were conceived to be machines (made up of only matter) then there could be no place for Soul. Omniscience was no longer the province of God. It was now the province of science.

Things were uncertain insofar as we lacked information. The drive for knowledge was the drive to eliminate uncertainty. In order to eliminate uncertainty, we were left with attempts to control as many variables as possible. The paradigm leads to control. Control the future, nature, workers, competition, everything. The methodology was consistent. Reduce things down to finer and finer components.

Something happened on the way to omniscience: Einstein happened along the way with relativity and quantum physics. In the subatomic world, it has been proven that uncertainty reigns. Heisenberg discovered the "Uncertainty Principle." Simply put, there will always be uncertainty. It is a **requirement** of reality.

If one understands that there can be no method that eliminates uncertainty, then a new way of thinking is required to make decisions. How can we be comfortable making decisions under unavoidable conditions of uncertainty? This is part of the new paradigm. We must learn to embrace and understand the limitations and possibilities that uncertainty suggests.

Quantum mechanics suggests that the universe is like an organism with all of its parts connected. The organic nature and interconnection of all reality is in stark contrast to classical mechanics. Quantum Physics places human perception at the heart of reality. An example can be found in the way light can be measured. Remembering back to your high school physics, a packet of light, or photon, is both a wave and a particle. These seemingly inconsistent aspects of reality will manifest themselves *only* when one chooses the method of perception! The experimental apparatus that one chooses to measure light actually determines the nature or reality of the photon. In other words, our perception determines our reality.

The quantum world-view places human consciousness at the center of our existence. If we are aware that everything in the universe is interconnected, then we have to realize that our actions are not isolated events, whole unto themselves. Our medical sciences must treat the whole body and not just isolated parts. This explains why the rise in holistic medicine is taking place. Corporate imperatives become global when the concept of an interconnected world is introduced. Our entire framework for understanding reality must reflect this new paradigm of "the whole being greater than the sum of its parts."

The new paradigm for science was brilliantly stated by Professor Stephen Jay Gould in his award-winning book, *The Mismeasure of Man*. If you replace the word "business" for "science," you will better understand the connection between the corporate world and a prevailing scientific ethic.

> "I believe that science must be understood as a social phenomenon, a gutsy human enterprise, not the work of robots programmed to collect pure information. Science...is a socially embedded activity. It progresses by hunch, vision, and intuition...Facts are not pure and unsullied bits of information; culture also influences what we see and how we see it. The most creative theories are often imaginative visions imposed upon facts; the source of imagination is also strongly cultural."

Just as the Soul was ripped away from Man by Newtonian mechanics, an organic framework makes Soul in everyday life once again possible. We can talk about values as part of our decision-making process. We can think not only with our mind but our hearts. After all, they are connected. We can let Soul enter our personal and professional decision-making. If we create our own reality by the act of perception, this enables and empowers us to truly make our dreams come true. This is true for both good and bad dreams. We also bear a responsibility for our consciousness. This responsibility for our perception extends even to our children. How we perceive our children may in fact create them.

The idea that perception creates our reality seems to violate common sense. Or does it? An experiment was conducted where grade school teachers were informed that "C" students were "A" students. These teachers perceived that these students were "A" students. The results were startling. The "C" students actually became "A" students, and many were transformed into top students long after they left the teachers in the experiment. The expectations and perceptions of the teachers created this new reality.

The move from a mechanistic paradigm to an organic, quantum model has a profound impact in the way decisions get made by corporate executives. We are in the midst of a paradigm shift. That does not mean that everyone marches in lockstep together operating under an enlightened decision-making process. It should become obvious from which framework corporations are operating when one examines the nature of decisions.

The new paradigm suggests that decisions should be made considering the totality of experiences and not reducing and isolating them from one another. Inter-departmental cooperation within an organization surfaces instead of competitive units. It is as if a new calculus is used in making decisions. An example of how the old paradigm and new paradigm contrast can be seen in the way Corning's breast implant and Johnson & Johnson's Tylenol tampering problems were handled.

For years Corning had reports that their breast implants may have been causing horrendous physical problems for many women. They responded by ignoring the problem **AND** continued business as usual. They made little effort to substantially change the product for years on end.

Johnson & Johnson, by contrast, responded to a tampering scare by recalling every bottle from the store shelves nationwide, redesigned their bottles and lost $70 million while seeing their market share shrink to almost zero. They felt a social responsibility and connection to their customers.

The results of both of the above speak for themselves. Corning declared bankruptcy after a class action suit brought a $4 billion-plus settlement while Tylenol recovered to regain the number one position in the nonprescription pain relief market.

Johnson & Johnson understood their responsibilities. They also understood that the value of their brand was worthless without connecting to their customers in a meaningful way. They exercised a long-term view of their business. Even though short-term profits were severely hurt due to the $70 million cost of the recall, they never wavered at all in the right thing to do. Even though they were uncertain if market share would ever be regained, they still did the right thing. They exhibited the definition of Corporate Soul.

But this new paradigm is not just for the large multi-national corporations. Corporate Soul at this point is found and exercised in entrepreneurial companies more frequently than their larger counterparts. It is the entrepreneur who uses his intuitions, passions, and vision almost daily. Every entrepreneur is faced with daily decisions of equal weight to those of Fortune 500 companies. This includes the dilemma between short-term gain versus long-term benefits. A significant aspect of corporate Soul deals with developing a time frame beyond immediate gratification.

An illustration from my own experience may serve as an appropriate example. Many years ago when working in a family business, the above particular issue arose. The family business happened to be my own family's. We were in the business of selling prerecorded videos to retailers and wholesalers all over the country. We had perfected the knack of creating artwork for the video box which almost guaranteed that the videos would be rented by consumers visiting retail stores. This meant that retailers would make money purchasing videos from us since the bulk of their revenues were garnered from video rentals.

There was one title in particular that did not live up to the promise of the artwork displayed on the box. The artwork had a vivacious, scantily-clad siren turning into a "beast." The video also had the distinction of being one of the worst films ever made...but it rented as if it was a blockbuster hit movie.

For a time we all congratulated ourselves for turning this sow's ear into a silk purse. The trouble was that everyone who rented the video was bitterly disappointed. They would inevitably complain to the store and eventually, I feared, we would get the backlash from angry store owners not trusting us. We could lose credibility with our customers. In some way we were violating that trust since the woman on the cover of the box was purely derived from an artist's imagination. She never appeared in the movie.

I began to tell retailers that our video was one of the worst films ever made and that if they ever purchased it from us, they stood a good chance of alienating their customers. I would politely suggest alternatives that would deliver to the expectations of the box cover art. An interesting note: over half of the retailers still purchased the video after my admonitions.

When my family heard this approach, an argument ensued. I did not know it then, but my family and I were operating under different paradigms. If one reduced the relationship with the retailer to the loss or profit gained from each interaction, then one course of action was "appropriate." Every opportunity to make money from each transaction was an independent event. Organic, interconnected thought deemed that in the long run, all transactions are related. The relationship supersedes any particular transaction. This was clearly a clash of paradigms.

Corporate Soul places a premium on relationships. To understand the interconnection of reality is to understand relationships. The whole notion of Soul itself implies something surviving the transaction or present. Is the Soul not eternal? It is this reason that Corporate Soul demands taking a longer-term view of conducting business.

Much has been written about CEOs compromising long-term strategic objectives for short-term, quarterly profits. We will come back to this point later. But if one believes that it is our perception and consciousness that creates reality, then by us becoming aware of our long term interests we will begin to create a reality in concert with those interests.

In this chapter, the words "new paradigm" have been used many times. As you may have surmised, it is hardly new. It has been around for over 70 years in mostly theoretical physics journals. What is new is attempting to apply the model to our thinking about organizational issues. Corporate America will accelerate the understanding of this paradigm once it becomes more fully understood.

It is also true that this paradigm can be applied to almost every type of institution we have. One will never be able to solve the crime problem simply by building more prisons. This is old paradigm thinking and not even very good old-time thinking. The problem is more complicated than this solution suggests. There are many interrelated issues comprising the problem. The war on drugs cannot be stopped by adding to the DEA budget tenfold.

The list of present problems in society requires a more holistic approach. We cannot continue to reduce things down to finer and finer components to get to the heart of problems. Too often this destroys understanding what you most want to understand. We need to discover the sometimes hidden relationships that often lead to resolving problems. It is a merging of science with art. It means letting Soulful activities enter your life.

One could write about educational Soul, political Soul, institutional Soul, etc., but the topic of corporate Soul offers the best chance for transforming society ever known to Man. Our economic system suggests that corporations have the potential for the largest impact for social change. Corporations cast their shadow over the world in more profound ways than all other institutions combined.

Religion once upon a time had this distinction and was a significant agent for change. But when they themselves surrendered Soul, it truly lost moral authority. Organized religion developed hierarchies, bureaucracies, and self-perpetuating dogma. It is ironic that the best hope for making Soul a widespread phenomenon is not religious institutions but corporations. We have entered a new millennium. It is not difficult to see the new paradigm taking hold. As the last millennium drew to a close, there was a sense of doom. Today we are filled with a sense of wonder and hope. Our destiny is in our own hands, heads, and hearts. They are connected. There is no more fitting way to end this chapter than a quote from one of Soul's most eloquent proponents,

"All of what you are doing in each day is creating what is appropriate and perfect. The shape of the experiences of your life is determined by the choices you make. It is you that chooses. Each choice that you make, to dwell in negativity or to take up residence in your heart, serves perfectly the evolution of the Soul. All roads lead to home."

--Gary Zukav, *The Seat of the Soul*

Chapter Two

Beyond the Zero-Sum Game

"Our Birth is but a sleep and a forgetting
The Soul that rises with us, our life's star
Hath had elsewhere its setting
And cometh from afar"
   --William Wordsworth

"Gordon, How much is enough?"

"It's not question of enough, pal. It's a zero-sum game. Somebody wins...somebody loses. Money itself isn't lost or made, it's simply transferred from one perception to the other."
   --Gordon Gecko, from the movie *Wall Street*

At some point in your life chances are you have become familiar with the Zero-Sum Game. I am not sure when I first became aware of this concept but have sure been a participant in the game too many times to count. It is a concept that is pervasive in everyday life.

Roughly translated, it means that a series of numbers added together will sum to zero. In more colloquial terms, it means one person's gain is precisely proportionate to another person's loss. We learn this "game" very early in our lives in the bosom of our family. If you have brothers or sisters, it is a good bet that if there were five pieces of candy and three siblings, someone was going to be shortchanged by one piece of candy, unless the oldest or strongest sibling managed to grab the entire mother lode of candy.

When there is scarcity, the Zero-Sum Game is most evident. If there is a finite quantity of anything, whether it is candy, money, power or even wins in a sporting event, then competition for these supposedly scarce resources takes over and creates the Zero-Sum Game. As we shall see, it is not always the case that scarcity is real. Often times we falsely impose the notion of scarcity when it does not apply. This is done sometimes consciously, as with the supposedly scarce commodity of oil during the embargo in 1973. Scarcity was manufactured to raise prices. Other times scarcity is created subconsciously. Here the perception becomes the overriding reality. An example of this is with personal power and energy. Many people attempt to hoard it because they feel that both are finite and scarce. The truth is quite the opposite as we shall explore in the "Passion and Energy" chapter. Personal power unfortunately takes the character of the Zero-Sum Game as it moves from "one perception to another." This is destructive to building Corporate Soul.

But in the competitive world of sports, winning a football game truly is a Zero-Sum Game. The winner wins at the expense of the loser. Unless there is a tie, all competitive sports have this zero-sum quality when winning is the only criteria of success. The Zero-Sum Game vanishes as soon as we modify the criteria for success. In a clash of competing teams, there is room for only one winning team. This is true scarcity. Competition feeds off this.

But as mentioned above if the criteria are changed, then even team or individual sports can move beyond the Zero-Sum Game. In Phil Jackson's book, *Sacred Hoops*, he writes,

"...I sensed that there was a link between spirit and sport. Besides, winning at any cost didn't interest me. From my years as a member of the New York Knicks, I'd already learned that winning is ephemeral. Yes, victory is sweet, but it doesn't necessarily make life any easier the next season or even the next day...In basketball--as in life-- true joy comes from being fully present in each and every moment, not just when things are going your way."

By changing one's perspective, one can move beyond "The Game." Joy is not a scarce resource. If one can develop the joy of being fully in the present moment, then regardless of the outcome, one can get satisfaction. This, by the way, does not hurt performance. It can actually improve performance; hence results. It is an irony that defies conventional thought.

It is not surprising that the Zero-Sum Game is pervasive in the corporate world. In fact, it *is* The Game. It is as if we believe that competition demands it. In point of fact, sometimes it does. In a mature widget market with no growth, one company's gain in widget sales can only be obtained at another company's loss. This is capitalism. This is competition. The finite nature of a mature market creates the perception of scarcity. The more mature the market, the more The Game is in effect.

In a growing market many companies can increase their business simultaneously. Sales, in this situation, are not part of the Zero-Sum Game. But we can impose scarcity by going to the next level: market share. This will always be a Zero-Sum Game because one company's gain is at the expense of another company's or companies' loss of market share. No matter how you try, nobody has ever figured out a way to grab 150% share of a market. Market share will always be finite and therefore scarce. Once again, this is the essence of what lies behind competition. This also shows that we can change the way we view reality by changing criteria--market share one way and gross sales another.

It is within this framework that The Game is played. We grow up with it in the family, our competitive games utilize it, and The Game pervades our economic system.

This Game is so ingrained in us that we develop strategies and tactics to come out on the winning side of the encounter. We see scarcity everywhere. But there is something that happens along the way. We begin to treat every encounter as if the Zero-Sum Game is the *only* game in life. Every situation becomes reduced to this game. Relationships within an organization take on a win/lose character regarding power. All negotiating takes on the same win/lose character of The Game.

But if we believe that there is a proper place for Soul in the corporate workplace, we must temper our most aggressive instincts and introduce fairness in our everyday dealings. We cannot treat every encounter in isolation from the entire relationship we are trying to create. The Game stems from our competitive nature and if we treat every encounter, deal or negotiation as a win/lose situation, then we may win the battle but also lose the more important overall war.

If you are a supplier and are negotiating a contract with a key client, it is clear that your gain is their loss. But do you really want to get the highest possible price for your goods or services? The word used in the above sentence was **highest** not best. The best price is not always the highest to an enlightened negotiator.

A stark example from history can serve as a vivid reminder. The treaty terms at Versailles after WWI were so "advantageous" to the allies and so detrimental to Germany (Zero-Sum Game at work) that as soon as Germany could do something about it, they did. World War II in a sense began with the terms extracted from a beaten foe. In the short term, it looked like extremely favorable terms for the Allies. They extracted the maximum price from their opponent. These terms were so good, they were disastrous for an entire world.

Back to the supplier scenario. It is incumbent upon you to look beyond The Game to develop pricing that is in the mutual, long-term interests of both you and your customer. This is certainly difficult. It is difficult to know where one's own best interests lie let alone the party on the other side of the table, as the WWI example clearly shows. Now you must take into consideration your customer's best interest also? But why not? Aren't you both connected in very real terms? If they go out of business, will this not effect you also? This is new paradigm thinking.

The hard-nosed among you might be saying, " If they are stupid enough to agree to unfavorable terms, maybe they should go out of business. If they do not know where their best interests lie, how can I or why should I even care?" I am reminded of something Sydney Greenstreet said to Humphrey Bogart in *The Maltese Falcon,*

> "Mr. Spade, men in the heat of passion are apt to not always know where their best interests lie...This calls for the most delicate of judgments."

Negotiating is filled with passion for many. There is nothing wrong with passion. It is an essential component of Soul. But one needs to be fully mindful of the present moment yet look beyond into the future. You need to see beyond the particular transaction. One needs to develop relationships based upon more than winning and losing. Companies that grasp this understand the value of relationships and will be able to compete in the next century more readily as the new paradigm takes firm hold. The new paradigm presupposes that we are all interconnected and when "the bell tolls," it tolls for all of us.

As a good supplier, you should always attempt to negotiate to the customers' needs, not their wants. When such a stance is taken, much of the negotiating takes on a different complexion. Negotiations become discussions about trends, mutual costs, inflation and how the relationship can move beyond the present boundaries to build and flourish. These are not Zero-Sum Game tactics. The parties involved are not entering into a ring like two Sumo wrestlers. They attempt to understand each other's needs.

The flip side of the coin is also valid. If you are the buyer negotiating with a supplier, naturally you want the best price you can get. Once again, the best price is not always the lowest price. Your suppliers have realities that need to be understood. Price is only one component of the relationship. There is always quality and service which often get shortchanged in negotiations.

As a large customer, you may be in position to dictate terms. You may strike such an aggressive deal that you plant the seeds for your own destruction. How many suppliers decided to skip a layer of distribution costs to recover the thin margins caused from overly aggressive customers? In this case, the customer creates his own competition by striking such a hard bargain.

It is important to consider what happens when economic realities create situations where mutual needs simply cannot be reconciled. If a supplier, due to his cost structures, cannot give a 65% discount and the customer, due to his cost structures, needs a 65% discount, then we have a situation of conflicting, irreconcilable needs.

When this happens, we see innovation in the marketplace. Sometimes we see mergers. It is precisely this tension that creates new relationships, new distribution methods and new, more efficient manufacturing techniques to meet the new necessities. Necessity is once again a parent to innovation and progress. We see the power of necessity time and time again. It is up to us to recognize this force.

One of the worst consequences of The Zero-Sum Game is the way it spills over to personal relationships within an organization. Building a team with a group consciousness is difficult (if not impossible) when each member is trying to gain advantage at the expense of the other team members. One needs to build a department or organization on the basis of selflessness. If everyone views every encounter with a win/lose mentality, then it is difficult to get people to believe in something greater than themselves. If you are trying to build a team, then you need to develop this group consciousness. Sam Walton was a genius in creating this awareness when his employees became "associates." This creates an identity that takes precedence over the individuals in a group.

In the final analysis, developing Corporate Soul requires a different perspective other than relationships predicated upon winners and losers. We cannot apply the same standards of competition and scarcity to all of our relationships. Transcending the Zero-Sum Game is necessary to developing a Soul in the workplace.

Chapter Three

Vision, Value, and Soul

"Soul is not a thing, but a quality or a dimension of experiencing life and ourselves. It has to do with depth, value, relatedness, heart and personal substance."

--Thomas Moore, *Care Of The Soul*

"My first act after being named head coach of the Bulls was to formulate a vision for the team. I had learned from the Lakota and my experience as a coach that vision is the source of leadership, the expansive dream state where everything begins and all is possible."

--Phil Jackson, *Sacred Hoops*

It makes no difference at what level you find yourself within an organization--one needs to develop a vision. This goes for the coach, entrepreneur, CEO, or line manager who must struggle often with competing visions from above as well as below. This is not a luxury but an essential component of leadership. Sometimes the notion of developing a vision is a source of derision. This usually emanates from those who turn a blind eye to its importance.

While running for reelection in 1992, George Bush criticized talk about the "vision thing." He was also routinely criticized for not having one, and he was the CEO of our country. He never really grasped what the criticism was all about. He was a captive of the old paradigm and would have been quite comfortable in the 18th century. There are many corporate executives in the same 18th century mindset today.

Although a great deal has recently been written about vision, often the nature of advice reflects an almost fast-food mentality to the problem. Just pull your car up to the drive-through window and place an order for a vision to go. The truth is that there is no simple way to develop a vision for your department, for your division, or for your company.

To develop an authentic vision, one must develop Soul. They are intimately linked. They both require understanding the past, *feeling the present* and projecting into the future. If a vision is to fit the organization, then it must be felt at every level of the organization. It is one of the biggest problems for any institution not to have a fully-developed and articulated, authentic vision. Some of the most successful proponents and practitioners of combining vision with Soul have been the great coaches in team sports. It is they who have crafted Soulful visions that have carried their teams to the pinnacle of success.

Confusion awaits the organization and executives who disregard developing a cohesive vision. So what do we mean by developing and articulating a vision? It is not just about making financial projections and budgets. It involves developing a sense of what your company is, what it stands for, and being able to communicate this within the organization.

The reason that vision and Soul are connected is that Soul clears vision. Soul is what makes the vision authentic. There are so many ways in which one's vision can be clouded. Of course there is the clouding of vision with drugs and alcohol. Have you ever witnessed the deluded visions of a "seer" under chemical influences? At best they are distorted.

There are even more deadly obstacles to clarity of vision. Having one's ego excessively involved with a plan makes a vision warped. How many CEOs have gotten their companies into new ventures because they fed an insatiable ego? When you see a merger of companies that are unrelated and are made to chase profits, vision with Soul is not at work. Ego-driven mergers rarely last. Soul requires a sense of selflessness that transcends ego.

Selfishness is a sure way to distort a vision. Because developing Soul means recognizing the interconnection of every part in an organization, selfishness is as foreign a concept as you can find. Connections and relationships nurture a group consciousness and this is one of the goals of a vision--to draw everyone toward a unity of purpose.

Many executives view vision analogous with a mission statement. They do not realize that a vision must go beyond a statement of objectives and be at the core of a management philosophy. Infusing a vision with Soul eliminates reducing it to a set of directives. The best coaches and executives understand that an authentic vision requires not only *what* should be done but also *how* objectives are to be achieved. Soul is the unifier. CEOs that have visions without Soul pit different divisions against each other to compete for scarce resources. "How" these leaders accomplish their tasks are suspect. What they actually do is create an atmosphere where no one will see or accept an overall vision for the company. Vision should work to unify an organization, not to exacerbate conflict. Vision with Soul seeks to transcend one's personal interest and see beyond that narrow self interest. I say right now there is no greater danger to a Soulful vision than allowing self-interest to run rampant, much less encouraging it.

Once again, we have old paradigm thinking because self-interest was thought to be the only principle for which one could count. If you are a CEO and your VPs are self-centered managers who prove incapable of developing a vision greater than themselves, it may be time to find some new VPs. Worse still, if you as an entrepreneur do not develop a philosophy that is beyond self-interest, the next century will not be kind to your business fortunes.

Developing a vision for the entrepreneur is critical to the long-term success of the organization. Entrepreneurs typically are blessed with enough passion to fill any room into which they walk. Desire and hope can at times interfere with an authentic vision. But a vision properly imbued with Soul can temper the excesses of desire. Often entrepreneurs seek to pursue any and all opportunities that come their way. If it will make money, then why not follow the passion? Pursuing an authentic vision may utilize passion but is not a slave to it.

Often all types of justifications can be made in the name of following one's passions and desires that do not necessarily synchronize with an authentic vision. Here the reductionist cost/benefit analysis can be used to rationalize the process. A hard-nosed accountant can make projections of future earnings and match those earnings against the costs associated with the opportunity. But if the "opportunity" does not coincide with the strategic vision, then one should seriously consider not pursuing this opportunity. This is even more dramatic for entrepreneurs because it is precisely this type of organization that has the scarcest of resources.

The allocation of scarce resources is one of the most critical responsibilities of both CEOs and line managers. Scarce resources should be martialed in pursuit of a Soulful vision. This does NOT mean that resources should always, by necessity, be allocated in pursuit of profits. We will discuss this later. How you decide to allocate resources is a way people in an organization learn about your priorities and get a glimpse of what your vision is. Whether you are a line manager or CEO, you will always be faced with allocating scarce resources, even if it is only your time. You can never forget that how you allocate your resources reflects what your objectives are and communicates these objectives within an organization. It is wise to avoid pursuing conflicting objectives when they create confusion.

A very apt cliché for pursuing conflicting objectives is, "...they just seemed to lose **sight** of their core business." Here the operative word is, of course, "sight." Potential profits are very seductive and often are the cause for shifting one's corporate objectives. The reason that Soul is such an important component in developing an authentic vision is that Soul considers profits but integrates this impulse with the broader concepts of value, Goodwill, responsibility, etc.

Simply put, vision with Soul most clearly helps steer one's organization through the multitude of opportunities that present themselves. As mentioned above, unchecked hope and desire create rash decisions along with the ever-present, ego-clouding vision with self-serving, short-term salves.

If one is going to develop an authentic vision, one must peel away the layers of issues that interfere with that development. One of the largest sources of interference with an authentic vision is the obsessive chasing after short-term profits. There are many CEOs that judge the performance of their business unit managers on quarterly profits garnered. Also, many CEOs themselves rise and fall with quarterly bottom lines.

Not only is this a ludicrous situation, but the health of an organization may also be compromised by this short-term view of business. Notice the word "view" which is an essential component of vision. It is difficult to compete in a world where your competition is making decisions based upon the long haul and you make decisions based upon looking at how they affect profitability only three months into the future. Many Japanese companies actually have a 100-year plan! Global competition demands longer term thinking.

Entrepreneurs often fall into the profitability trap. They do this in league with their banks who only care about the bottom line.

A banker once asked me how could it be that managing the bottom line in the short run could possibly harm a company. The answers are many. If one wants to throw out notions of social responsibility (illegally dumping toxic waste is a powerful way to improve short-term, quarterly profits), one is still left with an answer that needs to be made. Managing the bottom line is only one component to an owner or CEOs job. Increasing the **value** of their respective companies should be a much more powerful priority than short-term profits.

This concept provides a much broader compass for action. If one views personnel and the knowledge they possess as a valuable resource, one is apt to view downsizing a bit differently than those driven to quarterly profits. One manner of operating is long-term value centered, the other is short-term profit centered.

Let me say this again. The primary goal of a Soulful vision must be increasing the company's value. Often, short-term profitability concerns may actually interfere with increasing the **value** of one's company. Let me give three simple illustrations: an oil company, a motion picture company, and a mail order company.

An oil company makes money selling oil. They first have to expend huge resources prospecting for oil. Once they find a well, they must build derricks and pump the oil out in order to get it to the refineries. Each well has a finite amount of oil so they need to continually find new oil to keep the refineries busy and supply the market. As you may have guessed, prospecting for oil is one of the most expensive aspects about being in the oil business. The cost of sinking a new well that turns out to be a "duster" is monumentally high.

If a CEO of a large oil concern decides that short-term profits are the driving consideration in making decisions, one would simply stop prospecting and only pump oil from the existing wells. What would that do to the **value** of the company? First, oil reserves would go down, a major source of **value**. Second, future earnings would surely plummet due to an ever-decreasing volume of oil being pumped out and delivered to the market. But profits would be soaring! This CEO would be guilty of managing the bottom line in a march toward oblivion.

Of course if those profits were invested wisely, then a case could be made to do just this. But if the **value** is best measured by oil reserves and projected revenues from that oil, then the CEO would certainly be guilty of corporate malpractice. Remember this theme--we will come back to it.

Now let's take a look at a motion picture company. It matters little which ones we talk about, so we will use Disney as an example. What does Disney have to offer? First, there is the Disney name. This brand is recognizable and has come to mean quality children's programming. They also have a considerable library of classic films that will be popular forever. These are similar to oil wells, except each "well" or film will not run dry if properly managed. There is *Pinocchio, Cinderella, Jungle Book* and a host of others.

Before Michael Eisner came to Disney, the company was in trouble. Why? Well, they stopped drilling for new oil wells. They made fewer and fewer pictures and fewer and fewer television shows. They built theme parks, but their brand name was slipping into relative obscurity. They stopped making the films that had made them famous: animated classics. They began to reap the profits of the golden library, trying to manage the bottom line. Making a motion picture is as risky as prospecting for oil. If they could avoid the expense of prospecting for a "hit" motion picture, they could plow more of those profits into theme parks. Short-term profitability clashed head on with Walt's original vision.

The Disney name began to slip from public consciousness. From there, the brand's value began to decrease. Enter Michael Eisner, the oil magnate of the motion picture industry. He, as CEO, began drilling for new oil wells. He struck oil more than a few times and the **value** soared. He had an authentic vision for Disney. They started making animated feature films again. It is my opinion that the genius of Michael Eisner is in recognizing wherein the **value** of his company lies. The engine for everything that they wanted to do was creating quality programming that would enhance the Disney "magic."

But if you are an entrepreneur, does this theme still apply? Let's take a look at an entrepreneurial business like a mail order cataloger. Running a mail order business is a very capital-intensive, entrepreneurial operation. One of the largest components in the **value** of a mail order company is its database. One builds a database by prospecting for buyers. This prospecting is similar to the oil company prospecting for new reserves. To further carry the analogy, each prospect that purchases becomes a little oil well. Each purchaser has a certain amount of money that they will spend with you in their lifetime and therefore the total expected revenues decrease over time. The oil, in this case mail order revenues, depletes over time.

The lifetime **value** of a customer is as critical to the mail order company as oil reserves are to the oil company. As a database grows, there are more and more reserves to extract. The method of extraction is mailing additional catalogs to the buyers. If one wants to maximize the bottom line, one can stop prospecting for new buyers. Remember that prospecting is the most expensive part of the oil business, and it is with mail order as well.

What would happen if a mail order company stopped prospecting? Their short-term profits would be maximized but the march to oblivion would be on its way. The database would become depleted and the **value** of the company would be severely compromised, as well as future earnings.

Return to the banker for a moment. In fairness, he never used the words "maximizing the bottom line," but used the phrase, "managing the bottom line" to make his point. The above examples suggest that the time frames one uses has an effect on how one will manage or maximize the bottom line. If the **value** of a company is increasing exponentially and one's profits are flat, the owner or CEO is exercising valid, prudent business sense regardless of what the banker says. The job of the entrepreneur or CEO is to manage the **value** of the company and if done properly, profits are sure to follow.

The danger to the entrepreneur is surrendering one's vision to short-term profitability. As you may see by the above example, if you need capital from a bank, this might just be the case. Trying to share your vision and long-term view with old paradigm thinkers who reduce business to short-term profitability standards is a daunting task. If the increase in the **value** of the company is flat or decreasing and your profitability is questionable, then one has a different set of problems than described.

The word "value" has been put in bold type in the above discussion. The reason is that this is essential to understanding one's company and so intimately linked with vision and Soul. It is difficult to define; in fact it defies strict mathematical calculations. Often in a privately held company one learns what a company is valued at when someone is willing to pay for it. Even then, a company is "worth" different amounts to different companies.

Understanding wherein the value of your company lies can be a compass that continually steers your vision. That it is difficult to quantify this essential and elusive objective can be no excuse for ignoring it. One can not have a clearly defined vision without understanding value. The size of one's company truly makes no difference.

So far we have discussed how ego, selfishness, passions and obsessive adherence to short-term profits can compromise developing a Soulful vision. We have also discussed how understanding **value** and adopting a long-term perspective aids in the development of vision. Unfortunately there is no 12 step approach to developing vision. There is no science to it, but there is considerable art to developing an authentic vision. Art emanates from the Soul.

Having said this, there are things that every manager, entrepreneur, or CEO needs to do in order to create that specific, authentic vision. A friend of mine once told me that to clear one's mind and develop a vision, one needs to "create voids." Clearing one's mind is actually part of creating voids.

What does this mean? I suspect that it means freeing one from the daily onslaught of endless details. It is hard to conceptualize a vision when one is bombarded with information and responding to those details. It is almost as if the brain becomes overloaded with analysis and makes it difficult for the left-brain to work on a vision. Edward Bronfman, CEO of Seagram, warned that failing to create voids diverts attention from larger objectives. He said, "When you're up to your neck in alligators, it's easy to forget that you started out to drain the swamp."

Every manager who has worked their way up from the ranks knows that one problem in their possession is that they know too much. They know how to do the detailed work of their coworkers, and if they throw themselves into production, there is a good chance they will lose sight of the big picture. Planning becomes a difficult problem. Their view of the road is too close to the front bumper of their car. The faster the car moves, the more treacherous it is having their eyes close to the bumper.

Everyone needs to step back from the situation and create a void. The void more often than not will allow for solutions to present themselves. This freedom will allow the creative juices to flow and develop solutions to problems. It is as if creativity itself emanates from the void. Mozart was quoted as saying,

> "When I am, as it were, completely myself, entirely alone, and of good cheer--say, traveling in a carriage, or walking after a good meal, or during the night when I cannot sleep; it is on such occasions that ideas flow best and most abundantly. Whence and how they come, I know not; nor can I force them."

Not many of us are like Mozart, but the above quote hints at what the void is about. If you are a line manager, it will allow you to lift your head from the front of the bumper. The view will be one mile further down the road. This will allow you the luxury of planning for your department and creating solutions to the problems at hand.

If you are an entrepreneur, you are always dealing with so many issues. You deal with the banks, payroll, competition, customers, personnel, etc. This is not the most conducive environment for developing an authentic vision. You are probably overworked and do not spend enough time with your family. After working 70 hours every week, how much time is there to sit back, contemplate, and continue the dream that compelled you to start your business? Vision needs dreaming. Without this process, sterility will manifest.

Creating voids is about stepping back, clearing the mind, and integrating the dream with reality. One needs time for quiet contemplation for the Soul to reveal what is necessary. A void creates a vacuum in which things rush in to fill. The Soul rushes in to fill the mind's void. Developing an authentic vision requires imagination. The imagination needs unencumbered time to germinate.

If you are a CEO of a large concern, you too must create voids in order to develop a vision in concert with the Soul of your company. Often it is difficult to steer your organization in the face of competing internal business units. If you keep a social calendar that ensures mindless activity, you have to rethink what you are doing. It is your responsibility to combine vision with Soul, and creating voids in your life is one way to aid this essential process.

Once a manager, owner or CEO develops an authentic vision, then it must be carefully articulated within an organization. If a vision cannot be communicated, it becomes a source of bewilderment within an organization. In fact it can be a divisive force in an organization due to a lack of common understanding. Phil Jackson, the Zen-like coach of the Bulls said,

"...visions are never the sole property of one man or one woman. Before a vision can become a reality, it must be owned by every single member of the group."

If people do not share the same vision, it is similar to having a symphony with members playing different pieces of music. At best you will get a cacophonous sound.

Communicating a Soulful vision is not always an easy task. Just because you have come down from the mountain with a revealed truth does not mean that all of your legions will accept or even understand the strategic heartbeat of your vision. This is especially true if you have operated somewhat mindlessly in the past. It is also exceedingly difficult if your vision calls for a detour in direction. There is always strong resistance to change.

Resistance is sure to rear its head as entrenched agendas and competing visions conflict with your own. Even as CEO it is difficult if not impossible to impose your vision. A vision infused with Soul inspires acceptance. Implementing the directives of an authentic vision requires cooperation from all levels within an organization.

If one seeks to be more than a just a theoretical thinker, one needs to implement, in practice, the fruit of one's vision. That is why communication is a necessary component in the process of vision. Arnold Greenberg, the President of Coleco summed up his role as follows:

"My role is to be the ultimate inspirer, to dream the ultimate dreams, to see the vision, and impart that vision to others."

Developing a consensus regarding your vision is difficult. In doing this I am reminded of one of the best football coaches in the history of the game. A coach like the legendary Vince Lombardi grasped the notion of a Soulful vision and was able to communicate this within his entire organization. The Green Bay Packers of the Sixties not only had a common vision, they **believed**. It was Lombardi's responsibility to communicate his vision in a manner in which everybody could share, not just give lip service to an idea.

If you ever witnessed the beauty and precision of a Packer sweep, you would see perfection, harmony, and everybody acting together with common purpose. It made no difference what defense an opponent would use, they could not stop that sweep. Everybody knew their place in accomplishing their goals. Winning was not the most important thing. Understanding and sharing the vision was. Lombardi may have the distinction of being the most misquoted football coach in history. He is quoted as saying, "winning is not the most important thing...It is the only thing." He never said that. What he did say was, "Winning is not the most important thing...The **will to win** is the only thing."

The distinction in the above misquote and quote is profound. The **will to win** comes from deep inside. From one's character. From one's Soul. Vince Lombardi had a vision and was able to communicate in such a way to get everybody to share it. Even to this day, almost 20 years after Lombardi's death, his former players still revere him. Sharing a vision is almost a religious experience. It can actually transform individuals within an organization and certainly transform the organization itself. Placing the emphasis on the **will to win**, instead of winning, transforms an ordinary phrase into a Soulful endeavor.

Developing and communicating a Soulful vision considers the strategic assets one has at one's disposal. It may emanate from a dream but is also grounded in reality. Lombardi had the talent on the team to do the things he wanted to do. It was a combination of marrying the dream with the talents of that team.

Another prime example of connecting vision with Soul from the sports world is Pat Riley. As coach of the Los Angeles Lakers, he developed a team that will be remembered as having the best fast break in the history of the league. He developed a style that was most suitable to the assets of the team. Magic Johnson, James Worthy, and Kareem Abdul-Jabbar each played their role in fulfilling Riley's vision. His vision was deeply influenced by those strategic assets with which he had to work. Jabbar rebounded and fed outlet passes to a 6' 10" point guard who led the break with the swift moving Worthy crashing the lane.

When Riley left the Lakers to coach the New York Knicks, did he simply attempt to transfer and impose the same vision he had for the Lakers? He had won five world championships so one might think he would at least try. But Pat Riley's genius for his role made him understand that the resources at his disposal were different in New York than in LA. He had no dynamic point guard to lead the break. He had no swift forwards who could run the floor as if they were guards.

It took him time, but he developed a vision that utilized his new strategic assets. What were they? He had a center who was built like a Sherman Tank and could score from almost any place on the floor. He had power forwards that would go to war and his guards would hustle until they wore their opponents down to almost lifeless forms.

The Knicks became the best defensive team in either division. They intimidated their opponents and would win most games while scoring under 100 points. The style was polar opposite from the winning formula developed in Los Angeles. Pat Riley knew that he had to develop a new vision and that the Soul of his team could not surrender to a simple formula. There is no common formula that can fit every situation. One needs to craft a vision from the Soul of an organization.

Famed Renaissance painter/sculptor Michelangelo said that it was an artist's calling to liberate the figure encased in a block of marble. Pat Riley found a way to liberate the Soul of his vision encased in the collective spirit of each of his teams. His powers of communication allowed his teams to share that vision. One does not need to be a sports fan to appreciate the Soul at work and play.

So, too, it is for the corporate executive to understand the above experiences. It is a challenging endeavor to discover the particular Soulful vision encased in your organization. Once discovered, it is your duty to liberate that vision and allow the workings of the Soul to flower. When Pat Riley took over as coach of the Miami Heat, he was asked what style of play he was going to coach. He replied that it was going to take time to develop a style that fit the talents of his new team. Pat Riley fully understands the connection between vision and Soul.

Unless one can communicate that vision, it will be an impotent idea. An example of how a vision and communication skills can be a powerful combination is John F. Kennedy's 1961 speech. He dedicated our resources and inspired our nation to have an American step foot on the moon by the end of the decade. He developed a national shared vision, allocated scarce resources, and inspired a new future. On July 20, 1969, Neil Armstrong took, "...One small step for Man." Kennedy's vision survived his death.

The last significant quality of vision and Soul is inspiration. It matters little whether one is a coach, preacher, politician, line manager or CEO, one must lead and inspire those who follow. One's effectiveness depends on it.

Combining vision and Soul is a sincere voyage of discovery. It is a never-ending process through which you and your entire organization seize the future. It is an exciting journey well worth the time spent.

Chapter Four
Passion and Energy

"Passions are the only advocates that always persuade. A simple man with passion will be more persuasive than the most eloquent without."
--Rene Descartes

"Until they walk out on that floor and feel that excitement, that buzz, that energy, I'm just wasting my breath trying to capture that in words."
--Basketball all-star Joe Dumars

"Every great personality I have ever know who has demonstrated the capacity for prodigious work has been a person in tune with the Infinite. Every such person seems in harmony with Nature."
--Norman Vincent Peale

We are taught at a very early age that we must curb our passions and let reason guide our actions. Having interacted with hundreds of corporations in the course of my career, it appears that these lessons have been learned well. Our corporations reflect the way in which we think and feel, or the lack of both.

Generally speaking, our corporations have operated under the old paradigm of trying to think and be like machines. Machines do not possess passion. A workplace devoid of passion is a workplace devoid of a key attribute of Soul. It is generally easy to walk into a workplace and instantly know what energy level is present. Without passion, energy suffers. Energy is derived from passion. Without a proper energy level a corporation can wither away like a cornstalk in the Fall.

As the above quote from the great philosopher Descartes indicates, passion is an invaluable tool in sales and marketing. Passionate people who make their living persuading, which is exactly what salesmen do, will always be more successful than their passionless counterparts.

We all have met salespeople that bring excitement and energy to their presentation. These people are the most successful at their craft. Why? The reasons are many. One reason is that their excitement communicates that they believe in what they are saying. This goes a long way in convincing the other party that they should purchase what you are selling. Passion is more than excitement. It is a sincere expression of the Soul. When communication emanates from the heart, this is Soulful discourse and is a persuasive tool in a salesman's arsenal.

I have trained salesmen that had an excellent knowledge base and knew what to say but were unsuccessful. The *way* they communicated was the problem. They generally spoke in a monotone and were altogether unconvincing. Sales is about convincing. Business is about convincing. Passion is a way that transfers energy between buyer and seller and this transfer of energy is key in the buyer/seller relationship.

We all remember teachers growing up who would either display their passion for their craft or their contempt for their class. I remember a world history class that to this day sends me into drowsiness. Here I was, a student in love with history, excited about Roman Legions, The Crusades, The Inquisition, etc., yet the teacher so lacked passion for the subject matter that energy was actually sucked right out of my body!

Before we go any further, it is important to note that passion cannot be faked. It must be real. One of my first jobs out of college was as a door-to-door salesman. This was a tough job because every day one had to face the imminent prospect of rejection. Also it was important to get your "mind right." I could not fake passion for the product so I needed to learn about the product's benefits and only became successful once I began to believe in what I was doing.

I was the top salesman six months in a row and afterward was promoted to trainer. This is brought up not to brag but to contrast my miserable performance before I *believed* and after. Before becoming sincerely interested in the product, I was at the bottom of the hundred-plus sales force, making less than $100 per week. My eventual success was based upon my own transformation. It is empowering to know that we hold the keys to our own success.

As a trainer I discovered that there were too many people trying to be salesmen that didn't have "the juice." Some tried to fake passion, others simply hated their jobs so much that they would never devote themselves to mastering the art of sales. This is why it is important to align yourself and the people that work under you in positions that coincide with their talents and desires. If they do not fit, do not force them into positions that are bound to frustrate all parties concerned.

Passion is not just an important element in sales. It is an important element for the organization. One that requires new paradigm thinking to break the chains of utilizing reason alone. We are drawn to people with passion. They infuse us with an energy that makes us feel good. Managers that have passion generally have a quality called "charisma." This word means divine gift and favor. Wouldn't you rather be around a person that was endowed with a divine gift and favor? General George S. Patton Jr. said,

> "A man of diffident manner will *never* inspire confidence. A cold reserve cannot beget enthusiasm and so with the other [traits of success], there must be an outward and visible sign of the inward and spiritual grace."

This type of manager will generally be more successful than those without passion. More people than Patton have noted the importance of deportment. The great French novelist Voltaire said, "Any style that is not boring is a good one." The way you carry yourself is an indication of what is inside, a reflection of Soul...the inward and spiritual grace.

When people speak with passion from their heart, we tend to listen more and appreciate what is being said. We do not have to agree but often it is enough to appreciate what is being said for effect. Passion is not simply emotional intensity. It is caring and sincere. It is human. Gerry Spence is a famous lawyer/writer who stated in his book, *How to Argue and Win Every Time*, that the key to winning a courtroom argument was connecting with the jury...human to human. Sincerity and passion were his major tools. He has never lost a defense case in over 25 years of practice!

Corporations are in dire need of becoming more human. When we sit down to figure out what makes us different than machines and other animals, passion is something that sets us apart. When we rip this away from our personal or corporate endeavors, we tear away the very fabric of our Soul and that which makes us human. Introducing passion in the workplace is to introduce feelings into the work environment. This keeps us from becoming automatons and transforming workers into machines.

As mentioned in the chapter "Vision, Value, and Soul," we can not become a slave to passion. That is why we have fortunately been endowed with reason. But we need to recognize the significance of passion and its utility if we are to harness that energy from which it springs. It is similar to atomic power; it can be used for constructive purposes or destructive purposes. The path we choose is of our own making.

Passions are like reservoirs of energy to be tapped. If you are an athlete, it is the surge in energy created from the roar of a crowd. An artist gets an inspiration and loses himself in the work at hand. A corporate executive taps into this energy when a deadline is near and the hope and promise of a new product launch fills the atmosphere with a buzz. Why should we deny this? Everyone has experienced it, so let us bring it out of the cave and expose it to light.

Some executives hoard energy as if it were a *Zero-Sum* quantity. We possess an almost infinite amount of energy. Most of the time we do not have to apply standards of scarcity to this. Our movies have popularized the notion that energy is a scarce resource. In the movie *Cool Hand Luke*, Paul Newman portrays a rebel inside a prison. The inmates "feed" off his energy and he is quite comfortable with his role of leader. That is until he gets temporarily broken and yells, "Stop feeding off of me!" His reservoir went temporarily dry, but he recovered and built his energy back up to escape once more. Even after his murder he continued to enrich his mates from the grave. The memories of Luke sustained them.

As a leader you must be like a river and create an energy flow within your organization. There will be times that your reservoir will be lower than others. It is certainly ironic that the very act of infusing an enterprise with energy creates more in its void. The Universe with all of its matter and energy was created from a void and so you, too, can create energy from this void. Those times that you feel like screaming, "Stop feeding off of me," take a break to recharge. The act of "feeding" those around you will invigorate and replenish the reservoirs. The curious thing about energy flow is that when it is given freely, it is never draining. Only when you are less generous with giving it does the feeling of an energy drain occur. When we are fully engaged in an enterprise we almost always feel that we can go on forever.

People who hate their jobs are much more likely to be drained than those who work in jobs they love. If workers approach their jobs with passion, then they inevitably feel energized. Energy only seems finite to those who hoard it. They treat their passion and energy as if it was a commodity. Do not fall into the trap of turning the works of the Soul into a commodity. As long as the source of that energy is intact, your Soul will continue to nourish the enterprise. Good managers and CEOs instinctively give their energy freely.

One of the tragedies of today's managers is that they are so afraid of passion. Reason is the king to which they bow. Once again we are faced with a duality--passion versus reason. This is a western philosophical dilemma. Old paradigm thinking tells us to deny any validity to anything that does not spring from reason. New Age thinkers, on the other hand, discount reason altogether and suggest that the only valid method of understanding is experience and feelings.

Both ways of dealing with reality are just as wrong. They stem from an inability to synthesize these opposites. Eastern thought and modern physics have given us a framework to overcome this dilemma. Physics speak about attributes being complimentary. Light can be a wave and a particle. These compliment each other. It depends upon our frame of reference regarding the way we observe light to determine which aspect of light's nature is revealed. Physicists do not accept the either/or hypothesis when talking about light. Each method of description has validity.

We need to develop the language of Soul-speak like we developed the language of reason. We need to see how passion and reason compliment each other. To do this we need the advantage of different perspectives to elucidate our reality in more human terms. Many cultures have already done this.

Eastern thought speaks of "transcending" the dual nature of reality. We cannot ignore either aspect of reality. We must recognize its dual nature to understand the totality. It is precisely within our Soul that these dual aspects of nature play out. We must once and for all acknowledge the necessity of passion in the workplace. We must understand that passion is a way that Soul communicates with us and denying its role certainly denies an expression of Soul. When we deny this expression, we end up with a lifeless, machine-like corporate atmosphere that is disconnected with the world at large.

Good managers know that barriers break down when real human emotion is expressed among their troops. Passion is a connecting force. It brings people together. Why? It is certainly true that at the level of Soul, we are all connected. Jung called it the "collective unconscious" which is one way of saying that we humans all share some fundamental core attributes (archetypes in Jungian terminology). We are connected to each other by sharing DNA and also psychological characteristics. I suspect this is the reason that passion, an expression of Soul, brings humans together. A national tragedy like the Challenger explosion, the Oklahoma bombing, or the assassination of a president brings us together in a shared experience.

Some of the readers may be thinking that often passion is destructive. Heathcliffe in *Wuthering Heights* comes immediately to mind. What about anger, jealousy, avarice, hate? Passions are not relegated to love and positive energy. It is true that the full range of human emotions exist within the hearts and minds of all employees. To deny them is naive. But on a more instructive note, anger is not always the destructive force people believe it to be. Only when coming from a climate that represses its expression does it become destructive. It may initially be unpleasant, but it does not have to be destructive.

Also if passion is to have a role, it is not an exclusive role. What would happen if you became a slave to passion and threw any semblance of reason out of consideration? My guess is that you would have an erratic organization guided by excess. Reason must be employed with passion in developing a vision, developing a sales presentation, managing, and every other corporate endeavor.

I am not an advocate of "letting it all hang out!" We must get to understand the complimentary nature of reason **and** passion. We must overcome, transcend, synthesize or whatever else you wish to call it in order to have a balanced organization. This is not metaphysics but plain common sense. When we feel something, let us not ignore the feeling or push it into our subconscious. We cannot escape our humanness no matter how hard we try. We should not deny the feeling's validity, as this is the state of most modern corporate thinkers. If we have been programmed to believe that caring and feeling have no place in our corporate affairs, this can not serve us or society any longer.

As a entrepreneur, manager, or CEO, you are faced with the task of fostering the right energy flow within your organization. Creating an environment that stimulates creativity and energy is a proper goal. With our workers being asked to increase their productivity, it seems that the surest way to do this is to increase their energy level. It is not solely through your own abilities to communicate that this is done. Creating teams often enhances energy or even pairing of similarly talented individuals often creates sparks that spread throughout an organization. I have always believed that The Beatles and Monty Python created a special energy flow that resulted in increased output and creativity.

Equally important is the ability to ferret out those people within your organization who are "drainers." These people are usually very negative and suffer from a disposition that is selfish in all respects. I am sure we have all met people like this. They put down practically every idea and refuse to share their ideas or even potato chips in the lunchroom. Drainers actually look for opportunities to disrupt positive actions and feelings. They may do this by using the hard edge of reason to negate the positive vibrations within a group. It is difficult to explain in words all of the nuances of energy flow within an organization, but this does not mean you shouldn't try to get a handle on what is going on in your organization.

One day there will be a course taught at the Harvard Business School on "Energy Flow Within the Workplace." This will probably give the topic legitimacy among the Old Paradigm crowd. But anyone who has experienced the rush of energy and the drain of an unwanted grind already knows how it *feels*. As the language of the New Paradigm is being developed, we must address this vital force. To find the "nourishers" and the "drainers" is not that difficult once we know what we are looking for. At the very least you can detect the difference between the two by the effect they have upon the people around them. Encounters with drainers feel like you have just gone a few rounds with Mike Tyson. When you are around nourishers, you feel like the world has real possibilities. Hope springs from within as we are drawn to them. They create an environment that will help us cope with the world of uncertainty.

There is another agent of energy--the "poisoner." In many ways this type of person has learned to sustain negativity and pander to the dark side of human emotion. A poisoner typically spreads negative emotion on just about everything they touch. They rarely have any kind words and snipe away at ideas and people. Poisoners are among the most dangerous people within an organization since they reinforce everybody's negative energy and may actually supply temporary adrenaline rushes. Negative energy is inherently destructive and destabilizing to an organization.

"Poison" should be distinguished from sincere criticism. Critique is a product of reason while poison is a product of negative emotions. When a poisoner is found in an organization, it takes a large effort to turn this person around so they may utilize their energy in constructive ways. Ignoring them is harmful to the organization since they will wreak havoc preying on those around them.

We must face the future with our hearts and minds and not create our future with one to the exclusion of the other. I must admit that I do believe in the inherent goodness of Man and therefore feel less threatened in allowing the expression of Soul in the workplace. But the first step is to allow Soul to enter into your own decision-making process first. Let passion enter into your calculus when major issues are presented. Foster a positive environment that will increase the energy level within your organization. I am sure that you will find the experience personally as well as professionally rewarding.

Chapter Five

Marketing with Soul

"You tread the ridge between truth and insult with the skill of a mountain goat."
  --Crasseus, from the movie *Spartacus*

"When all hearts are opened,
And all the secrets known,
When guile and lies are banished,
And subterfuge is gone"
  --Patton, the opening verse from his poem, "Valor"

"Anybody who tries to make site determinations mathematically, by charts, or by other scientific methods is wrong. It's that vast body of experience that you retain in your brain and pull out as you need it that's important in picking winners."
  --Trammell Crow, one-time CPA and real estate developer

In all too many cases the coupling of these two words--Marketing and Soul--seems like an oxymoron. One need only to look at the billboards of the Marlboro Man or Joe Camel to see evidence of the separation of Soul from marketing. Look at your mail closely and see if you receive anything in May that looks suspiciously like an IRS check, only to be a solicitation from a car dealer. Watch an old-time movie like *The Hucksters*, starring Clark Gable or comb through late night television and see 30 minute Infomercials promising everything from cures for balding to instant wealth. You may soon get the notion that Soul and marketing are mutually exclusive ideas.

If many attempts at marketing are not outright attempts at deception, they often tread the line between truth and deception with the same skill as the mountain goat of *Spartacus* fame. So, if marketing with Soul is so important, why do we have so many examples of outrageously Soulless campaigns around us?

Deception has been around since the dawn of time. This often works as a short-term strategy because the message is always aimed at a human weakness: greed, vanity, pride, ego, etc. These strategies have brought results. If marketing strategies do not work, they are quickly discarded. So if you are responsible for marketing and being judged by the results, should you even think about this Soul "thing?" The answer: ABSOLUTELY!

The simple answer is that times are changing. What worked in the past will not continue to work in the coming millennium. Marketing people are instinctively experts in psychology. They have to be. They must be masters at what will motivate a potential consumer to purchase. It should not escape everyone's notice that consumers are going through a transformation. We are faced with an increasingly skeptical and cynical public. If we want to succeed at marketing in the future, then it is important for us to explore the source of this discontent.

We must acknowledge that we are experiencing a crisis of confidence. Less than 60% of eligible voters actually cast their ballot. Why don't we vote in greater numbers? We have a name for direct mail marketing messages: junk mail! What makes this mail junk? We possess remote controls that allow us to change channels at the first hint of a commercial. My wife sometimes believes I have thumb seizures when the remote is in my hand. Why do we evade these commercials so feverishly?

The same reason that we do not vote, answer junk mail, and change channels during commercials is part of the same phenomenon--the messages all too often lack Soul. They lack a sense of true, authentic connection with us. Most of our junk mail does not speak to us for if it did, we wouldn't dream of calling it junk. The solicitations that do speak to me are not "junk," they represent opportunities. Commercials that reach down and touch something special inside as well as entertain me, arrest my thumb from remote madness. Politicians that speak to us in more than prepackaged, six-second sound bytes and deliver real inspiration could move an electorate enough to take to the polls.

Marketing without Soul has created a public without trust. Any marketing strategy that feeds this cycle of mistrust will inevitably fail as we edge closer and closer to a public deep with disgust. Even our nightly news programs foster our cynicism by continually marketing images and stories that appeal to our base instincts. We are now near critical mass regarding the public's cynicism. We will certainly reach it in the near future. When this happens, the old way of mass marketing must give way to a better way of relating to our target audience.

We have grown used to the idea of exclusively relying on repetition of a marketing message instead of the quality of the message. We would rather irritate and pander to base instincts than expose the Soul of a product or Soul of a message. The product does not have to be noble to market with Soul. One of the greatest campaigns in history belongs to Budweiser who had a series of absolutely gorgeous, scenic commercials of Clydesdale horses pulling a sleigh set to holiday music.

I would never exercise my thumb when one of these spots interrupted my viewing. In fact, the commercials became part of my viewing. Recently I was in a meeting in which a television was on in the background. A Budweiser commercial featuring an alligator swaggering to reggae music appeared. The alligator had a case of Budweiser and three frogs on his back and was "jammin". The meeting stopped with the words, "Have you seen this great commercial?" This spot stopped the meeting! This was their intention--to connect with the viewer. They succeeded. In both examples, the marketer found a Soulful way to market a product that traditionally panders to our less noble side.

If you are marketing a product with absolutely no socially-redeeming qualities, can you still market with Soul? The industry that first and foremost comes to mind is the tobacco industry. While they are guilty of soulless marketing most of the time, occasionally even they have stumbled upon a campaign with Soul. Do you remember the campaign that featured the Declaration of Independence and the Constitution? The industry mounted a campaign to mobilize voters and consumers to assert their rights of freedom. Their message was **freedom from** government interference and **freedom to** live or die as we see fit. The message had Soul and even connected with me, and I am an ardent anti-smoker.

A departed friend of mine, Frank Zappa, once told me that the essence of today's marketing boils down to one thing: Promise that by purchasing any product, the buyer will have great sex. While this is overstated (and cleaned up for the reader), it does have more than a grain of truth to it. Titillation and sex in advertising are much more common than the promotion of sincere relationships and love.

If a message is repeated often enough, then it permeates to the subconscious level. At this level some actually believe that smoking is a virile pursuit, that drinking a beer with a bikini-clad model will win her over, that the right kind of underarm deodorant will ensure the man of your dreams, the right kind of car leads to bachelor heaven.

As far as this chapter is concerned, it does not matter what the product is that you are trying to sell. Although in a different context you may want to reconsider working in an industry or marketing a product in which you hold contempt. You will be faced with many decisions. To what are you going to appeal? Are you going to attempt to build trust between your brand and the customer? Are you going to build a relationship that transcends the transaction? Are you going to communicate the intrinsic value of your product or go negative toward your competition?

The whole concept of marketing with Soul is about uniting the marketing means with the results desired. It is an empty, Soulless enterprise to achieve one's ends at any price. The following example, quoted in the book, *Flow*, is about a Naples antique store owner and illustrates this principle,

"One morning a prosperous looking American lady walked into the store, and after looking around for a while, asked the price of a pair of baroque wooden *putti*, those chubby little cherubs so dear to Neapolitan craftsman of a few centuries ago, and to their contemporary imitators. Signor Orsini, the owner, quoted an exorbitant price. The woman took out her folder of traveler's checks, ready to pay for the dubious artifacts. [Signor Orsini] turned purple and with barely contained agitation escorted the customer out of the store: 'No, no *signora*, I am sorry but I cannot sell you those angels.' To the flabbergasted woman he kept repeating, "I cannot make business with you. You understand?' After the tourist finally left, he calmed down and explained: 'If I was starving, I would have taken her money. But since I am not, why should I make a deal that isn't any fun? I enjoy the clash of wits in bargaining, when two persons try to outdo each other with ruses and eloquence. She didn't even flinch. She didn't know any better...If I had sold those pieces to that woman at the ridiculous price, I would have felt cheated."

Signor Orsini loved the process of selling. It was his craft. The means (outdoing each other with ruses and eloquence) was as important as the end game--the sale. In fact, he did not separate them in his mind. He did not and would not (unless he was starving) separate the means and the end. He practices his craft with Soul and thus derives a great deal of pleasure from each and every transaction.

Marketing with Soul also means having respect for your audience. It is not necessary to insult or demean at every turn. Real respect will make you approach the delivery of messages with integrity. If you want to build trust, you need to have genuine integrity in communicating. Relationships, whether personal or business, that are founded on anything less will not be sustained. If you give respect, you are likely to get the same in return. Trust is one of the hardest things to gain and one of the easiest things to lose. Take care to nurture those seeds of trust whenever planted.

In order to market with Soul, one needs to bring passion and energy to the craft. One must understand that connecting with the buyer creates a relationship that will last after the transaction is completed.

Building relationships is an integral part of Soul. It is about finding creative ways to allow our better natures to flower. Marketing with these values behind the effort yields a soulful campaign.

It is at the level of Soul that the interconnection of all of humanity becomes manifest. Getting insight into this "collective mind" is an important element in marketing since fashion and trends reflect this collectivity. Marketing into one of these trends can be an extremely profitable enterprise. The successes of the Hula Hoop, Cabbage Patch Doll, and Pet Rock verify how fortunes are made marketing to the collective mind.

This is not metaphysical nonsense. Many people believe that the above examples are simply cases where the marketers were just plain lucky. We must not forget that we make our own luck and at the very least we have to be prepared to seize upon it. Devaluing the genius, and intuitive impulse of bringing the

Hula Hoop to market by relegating it to mindless luck is just plain wrong. Something in the marketer of the Hula Hoop connected to a collective impulse that transcended the product. This is what can happen when Soul and marketing are combined.

Marketing with Soul cannot exclusively use quantitative measures, such as focus groups, polls, regression analysis, etc. to become acquainted with the collective mind. The methodology lies outside a rational process reducible to numbers. The spark of discovery comes from intuitive powers that emanate from deep within one's psyche, or Soul. Marketing with Soul uses intuition to sense in which ways the consuming herds are likely to turn. Nuclear physicist turned marketing executive, Solomon Dutka explains:

> "Your own universe determines the kind of intuition you need. The scientist struggles to unlock nature's secrets. But nature is passive and uncapricious. It doesn't take advantage of a missed opportunity. The businessman struggling to make a buck in a chaotically competitive arena faces capriciously changing demographics. He's suddenly out of business if he doesn't *sense* the right thing to do."

We have been saying that at the very core of our being, the shared psychology of all Mankind is revealed. Learning to market with Soul leads to understanding not only one's self but others as well. Marketing with this kind of understanding takes on a completely different emphasis. We try to find the quality or qualities of a product that satisfy the needs or desires of that collective mind in which we are all participants.

Our marketing does not just reflect what the consuming public wants. It also creates the atmosphere of desire. One cigarette company which had green packaging was thinking about changing the color to better appeal to the day's favorite fashion color. They thought sales would go up if the color of its packaging would not clash with clothing. Instead of changing the color of their packaging, they decided to spend millions of dollars in making green the fashion color of choice.

It is absurd to think that we "only give the public what they want." Consumer desires not only create the fodder for successful campaigns, but they reflect the genius of a marketing campaign. It is a mutually reinforcing loop. As stated earlier, consumers are growing increasingly skeptical. We are nearing critical mass when it comes to the public's disgust with hucksterism, deception, pandering, etc. Marketing with Soul can never be outdated and soon will be essential for success. When the critical mass of disgust is reached, the explosion will be heard by every marketing department in the country.

When marketing with Soul becomes part of the new business paradigm, then a positive reinforcing loop will actually nourish the consumer. This in turn will create a bond that is difficult to break between you and your customers. Creating a solid, unbreakable bond between you and the customer is the essence of building a brand and hence a business.

A story about my father illustrates this lesson well. He owned his own small company that imported carbide-tipped saw blades from Sweden and sold them to cabinet makers all over the Midwest. He also serviced the saw blades, picking them up when the tips were dull, and sharpening them. One day one of his larger customers had a horrendous fire. Having so much wood in the place, the inventory was wiped out and most of the machinery, and saw blades, were destroyed. To make matters worse, the company was underinsured.

The owners of this company had grit and decided to continue. One week after the fire my father took an entire set of saw blades and router bits to them and simply said, "I know you can't pay me now. You can pay me after you get on your feet, until then, don't worry about it."

An unspoken bond was created that never was broken. This cabinet company recovered and grew to become the largest in Illinois. They never bought a saw blade or router bit from anybody else until my father sold his business. At the risk of sounding like a proud son, my father exhibited Soul in his business relationships as well as life. When Soul enters your life, it also enters into your business affairs with the reverse just as true. Soul is truly difficult to compartmentalize into various roles of your life.

In the last chapter the importance of passion was outlined. In Descartes's words, "...a simple man with passion will be more persuasive than the most eloquent without." Being a great marketer will come naturally if one has conviction and its cousin, passion. One does not need an abundance of eloquence. Authentic, sincere communication infused with energy is the well from which to draw the water when designing a campaign.

Having passion, conviction, and enthusiasm for what you are marketing will lead to a natural outpouring of Soul. Norman Vincent Peale described the secret of a politician who had been "marketing" his message in a series of seven speeches in one day without so much as tiring:

"That's the secret. He was on fire for something. He was pouring himself out, and you never lose energy and vitality in so doing. You only lose energy when life becomes dull in your mind. Your mind gets bored and therefore tired of doing nothing...Get interested in something! Get absolutely enthralled in something! Get out of yourself! Be somebody! Do something...The more you lose yourself in something bigger than yourself, the more energy you will have."

Wouldn't you want someone on your marketing team who thinks in a similar manner as captured in the above quote? Allowing Soul to enter into every phase of the corporate enterprise breeds so many positive effects and will even spill into the inanimate objects you are marketing.

Marketing with Soul is all-encompassing. It truly involves understanding the totality of the corporate experience as well as the connection between the consumers and that company. The company and the consumer become partners in a relationship that should seek the high ground. This is the kind of marketing that will lead us beyond today's cynicism and help build a healthy society based upon trust.

Chapter Six

Responsibility and Soul

"The President in Washington sends word that he wishes to buy our land. But how can you buy or sell the sky? The land? The idea is strange to us. If we do not own the freshness of the air and the sparkle of the water, how can you buy them?

"Every part of this earth is sacred to my people. Every shining pine needle, every sandy shore, every mist in the dark woods, every humming insect. All are holy in the memory and experience of my people.

"We know the sap that courses through the trees as we know the blood that courses through our veins. We are part of the earth as it is part of us. The perfumed flowers are our sisters. The bear, the deer, the great eagle--these are our brothers. The rocky crests, the juices in the meadow, the body heat of the pony, and man, all belong to the same family.

"The shining water that moves in the streams and rivers is not just water, but the blood of our ancestors. If we sell you our land, you must remember that it is sacred. Each ghostly reflection in the clear waters of the lakes tells of events and memories in the life of my people. The water's murmur is the voice of my father's father.

"The rivers are our brothers. They quench our thirst. They carry our canoes and feed our children. So you must give to the rivers the kindness you would give to any brother.

"If we sell you our land, remember that the air is precious to us, that the air shares its spirit with all the life it supports. The wind that gave our grandfather his first breath also receives his last sigh. The wind also gives our children the spirit of life. So if we sell you our land, you must keep it apart and sacred, as a place where man can go to taste the wind that is sweetened by the meadow flowers.

"Will you teach your children what we have taught our children? That the earth is our mother? What befalls the earth befalls all the sons of the earth.

"This we know: the earth does not belong to man, man belongs to the earth. All things are connected like the blood that unites us all. Man did not weave the web of life, he is merely a strand in it. Whatever he does to the web, he does to himself.

"One thing we know; our God is your God. The earth is precious to him and to harm the earth is to heap contempt on its creator.

"Your destiny is a mystery to us. What will happen when the buffalo are all slaughtered? The wild horses tamed?

What will happen when the secret corners of the forest are heavy with the scent of many men and the ripe hills are blotted by talking wires? Where will the thicket be? Gone! Where will the eagle be? Gone! And what is it to say good-bye to the swift pony and hunt? The end of living and the beginning of survival.

"When the last Red Man has vanished with his wilderness and his memory is only the shadow of a cloud moving across a prairie, will these shores and forests still be here? Will there be any of the spirit of my people left?

"We love this earth as a newborn loves its mother's heart-beat. So, if we sell you our land, love it as we have loved it. Care for it as we have cared for it. Hold in your mind the memory of the land as it is when you receive it. Preserve the land for all children and love it, as God loves us all.

"As we are part of the land, you too are part of the land. This earth is precious to us. It is also precious to you. One thing we know: there is only one God. No man, be he Red Man or White Man, can be apart. We *are* brothers after all."
    --Chief Seattle, in a letter to the President in 1852

When I first came across these powerful words, I sat with dumbstruck awe. Who was this man? It reads as if written yesterday yet was sent to our President almost 150 years ago. There is no greater exposition of Soul and no greater outline of environmental and social responsibility than from the pen of the great Native American, Chief Seattle. Were these words only a heartfelt expression of a proud leader on the verge of seeing his world crumble before his eyes, it would neither head this chapter nor grace the pages of this book in any place. But we see in these words the Soul of a leader and his keen understanding of our responsibilities that extend beyond the environment. We must examine these words a little deeper. We see in this letter his keen understanding of not only how we are all interconnected with each other as human beings, but also how we are connected with Nature.

This understanding is in harmony with the topic of this book. We should take note that although the sentiment expressed throughout Chief Seattle's letter may be a guiding beacon toward the new paradigm for business, it has been around as a philosophy of life for some time. Its tenets are well stated. Not only are we all connected with each other as people, in a dance of intertwined genetic and psychological realities, we are significantly connected to the rivers, the trees, and the air we breathe.

Accepting the premise of connection is the first step to understanding what our responsibilities are to our fellow man, fellow workers, and the environment that nurtures our very existence. For how can we dump toxic waste into our oceans and rivers when we understand the Soulful connection between us? How can we pollute the very air that we breathe if we believe that from it springs the spirit of our children? We could no more burn down our siblings' homes than destroy a forest if we believed that the animals that dwell under its protective canopy are also members of our family.

While this may ring sentimental to many readers, if one accepts the notion of interconnection then the conclusions are inescapable; we must accept responsibility on many levels.

Interconnection means that our actions affect more than ourselves and that it is we who create our world. Responsibility can be seen as a series of concentric circles. We have responsibilities to our family, fellow workers, shareholders, country, and even Nature.

We have a responsibility to Mother Earth. She has nurtured our ancestors as she continues to sustain us. If we take care of her, we will bequeath an important resource for generations to come. If we approach Nature with disregard, or worse, contempt, will it sustain us forever? We must always remember that what we do to our environment, we do to ourselves as well. Can we deny this simple truth?

We have a responsibility to treat our subordinates with respect and dignity. Not only will it likely be returned in kind, but it also makes for good business. It may not always be easy, but offering sincere respect and understanding to subordinates will have its positive ends. We need an education system that imparts the worth of our fellow man so this form of interpersonal communication becomes the standard way of relating.

We have a responsibility to the shareholders. This means much more than chasing after short-term profits. We need to develop criteria that takes into consideration the value of intangibles. We need to develop a reward system that has concerns for and is infused with Soul. We need to take into consideration our contribution to the welfare of something greater than ourselves. Ben & Jerry's company understands this and I believe that its overall corporate philosophy and attention to the environment and values is reflected in the value of its Goodwill. They seem to know that if we devalue Nature, we devalue ourselves.

We need to develop a corporate environment that does not run away from responsibility but embraces it at the heart of every experience. Responsibility goes beyond blame. This means that we must foster that idea that most mistakes are simply not so critical that termination looms just around the corner. Evading responsibility is so pervasive it has become a national epidemic and not just a protective umbrella for middle management. It has become acceptable to pass the buck, so much that a jury awarded a six figure dollar amount to a lady who spilled coffee in her lap while going through a drive-through at McDonald's. The coffee was hot! She managed to evade personal responsibility even though she was carrying the coffee between her legs while pulling away from the drive-through window.

The collapse of personal responsibility in our society is everywhere. We see it in attempts to explain away crime by evoking Skinnerian, behavioralist conditions. We see it in school administrators explaining their district's low test scores after reading The Bell Curve, which frees them from responsibility due to genetics. We see it in a divorce rate that disconnects the partners from responsibility to a unit higher than themselves: the family. We see it in men who refuse to own up to their responsibilities as fathers and leave behind unwed mothers or worse, abortions. The list could go on and on. It is no wonder that we hardly even know what the concept is. Once upon a time it was natural to understand responsibility. Now we must study what was once natural.

If our society is to the point of awarding a drive-through customer money to evade her personal responsibility, something is very wrong. It is just as bizarre to have a work environment within an organization that punishes those who accept responsibility. Yet most corporations reward evasion of responsibility.

We have all seen organizations that encourage disclosure of problems only to be followed by condemnation heaped upon the disclosing person. Needless to say, this does not enhance or foster subordinates to bring problems out in the open. It would be like telling your children not to lie and then as soon as they disclose the truth about one of their wrongdoings, they would be spanked for the indiscretion. This hardly encourages further truths and actually encourages children not to own up to their responsibilities.

I am not suggesting that as a manager, entrepreneur, or CEO that you should never discipline or fire someone. It is just that one needs to assign responsibility, build it, foster it, **before** results are judged. Responsibility must be more than a tool used to assign blame when things do not go quite right.

This leads me to another style of management dealing with responsibility. You will not learn about it in business school. I call it the "Catch 22." Taken from the book of the same title and applied in the corporate environment, it goes something like this: assign someone a task for which they are entirely responsible. When the fruit of their responsibility is ready to be eaten, dismiss it altogether. Then a reprimand is given because the task was not done. In a "Catch 22," someone is responsible to the extent that their conception of the task coincides with management's ideas, otherwise it is rejected summarily.

True responsibility can only be assigned once the assignee has the right to be wrong. Obviously there are many decisions that could be made in which a wrong decision could spell doom for an organization, but certainly this is not the case with every decision. This will be explored in the "Management and Soul" chapter at length.

The above example hints at something profound--the link between freedom and responsibility. I have never worked in an organization in which the rank and file did not yearn for more freedom. **Freedom from** silly rules as well as **freedom** to do their jobs. Rarely is the close companion of freedom--responsibility--yearned for as much. In fact, the connection between the two has been lost.

Your job as an executive is to rediscover the connection between these two powerful concepts and infuse the organization with their true meaning. If you are a manager who wishes to control every minute detail of every subordinate, do not be surprised if they will not accept responsibility. You are to blame, and not them, for the lack of initiative. Likewise, if you are a manager who does not want to control your troops, who believes in freedom, but will not allow true responsibility to flow downward, then the results are the same. You will reap an uninspired group.

One style wants to control the process while the other wants to control the end result. Each style is a controlling style and does not connect freedom and responsibility.

There are so many times in an executive's life that one is faced with seemingly conflicting responsibilities. These conflicts usually arrive from either a lack of values or a failure in understanding the nature of those concentric circles of responsibility. If one has no family, one is not apt to understand the responsibilities attendant with having one. Unfortunately there are too many of our corporate executives lacking Soul and have not developed the skills needed to resolve seemingly conflicting responsibilities.

This leads to surrendering to one set of objectives or responsibilities to the exclusion of all others. Hence, a short-term "solution," like polluting our environment because it is "cheaper" than other alternatives, becomes an all-too-easy course of action. The water is further muddied when the decision maker is responsible for lowering costs. We all too often slip into a bipolar world of seeing everything as an either/or situation. No pair of opposites are irreconcilable. It is up to us to find the right perspective from which to view the duality. We need to have all our faculties of reason, all of our heart and Soul, mobilized to face up to our myriad responsibilities. That is why we need to read Chief Seattle in our business schools, for he engages our heart, spirit, and reason in the understanding of our world. Reading his words seems prophetic yet we also know that our destiny is of our own making.

Allowing Soul to enter into our corporate affairs is an all-encompassing endeavor. It means allowing it to flower in our decision-making, our relationships with our coworkers and subordinates, our suppliers and customers, our environment. We must develop a sense of reverence to things greater than ourselves. Once this is accomplished, there is no doubt about our corporations becoming more responsible. Responsibility flows from values, from Soul.

Chief Seattle gives us a guide to a value system that connects us to something larger than ourselves: Nature and our fellow Man. His is a language of living and not merely surviving. His stirring words can help develop a framework from which corporations can encourage freedom and responsibility as the Soul of a company emerges.

Chapter Seven

Management and Soul

"I am sure that if every leader who goes into battle will promise himself that he will come out either a conqueror or a corpse, he is sure to win. There is no doubt of that. Defeat is not due to losses but to the destruction of the Soul of the leaders--the 'live to fight another day' doctrine."
   --General George S. Patton Jr.

"Okay, we've got two minutes. You know what it is going to take. It is going to take your best effort on every play. Dedicate ourselves to that and we should have no problems. Go out and play Bear football, smart and aggressive. If something bad happens, don't worry. Why? Because we're in this together as a football team and we are going to play it for each other. We are going to win it for each other and we're going to pick each other up. That's what it's all about. This is your game. Any other intention won't be accepted."
   --Mike Ditka's pre-game speech, Super Bowl XX

**"I've learned that the most effective way to forge a winning
team is to call on the players' need to connect with something larger than themselves. Even for those who don't consider themselves "spiritual" in a conventional sense, creating a successful team--whether it's an NBA champion or a
record-setting sales force--is essentially a spiritual act. It
requires the individuals involved to surrender their self-
interest for the greater good so that the whole adds up to
more than the sum of its parts."**
--Phil Jackson, from his introduction in *Sacred Hoops*

There is no easy description or guide on how to combine Soul
with management. The one constant throughout this book is
that there are no easy, quick fix answers to corporate problems.
The nature of this entire text is more akin to an inquiry written
to stimulate thinking in the hopes that each reader can search
their own path to a personal and professional life infused with
what we are calling Soul.

The above quotes came from three leaders who were and are
acknowledged in their respective fields for being special. Each
of their management styles were completely different, yet each
reached heights for which only few dream. But they had many
great qualities in common: they accepted responsibility, they
cared for their subordinates, and these leaders dared to lead!

What do I mean by daring to lead? I mean above everything
else that whether you are a coach, commander in the armed
forces, manager, or CEO, you must take the step to be strong
enough to reveal yourself to the group you are leading. Patton
said, "As a mirror shows us not ourselves, but our reflection, so

it is with Soul." We reflect our Soul in the way we go about leading our family.

I always thought a good model of leadership and management was the family model. Raising three sons, one of my major responsibilities is to prepare them for the day when they will strike out on their own without my active guiding hand. This means that it is my responsibility to teach them, yet give them enough independence so they can learn how to make decisions.

As a manager you also must prepare your subordinates for making decisions without your active guiding hand. You need to develop in your troops initiative, for if you do not, there will certainly be a limit to growth. Preparing the way for subordinates not to need you is threatening to most managers. Phil Jackson in *Sacred Hoops* states:

> "Some coaches feel threatened when their players start asserting their independence, but I think it is much more effective to open up the decision-making process to everybody...The players often have a better handle on the problem than the coaching staff because they're right in the thick of the action and can pick up intuitively the opposition's strengths and weaknesses."

We have all seen managers who will not allow subordinates to make any decisions. They rationalize that only they as managers are gifted with the right answers. Soliciting advice from subordinates who are in the thick of the situation is one of the most underutilized sources of wisdom in an organization. The Japanese seem to grasp this much better than their western counterparts. They view all the people within their organization as valuable precisely because each person has knowledge valuable to the corporation. It is the job of managers to liberate this knowledge and add it to the common knowledge pool.

As a parent, one of the hardest things to face is allowing your children the right to be wrong. Certainly their rights change as they grow and become more responsible. George Carlin had a comedy routine that I still quote often. He talks about RULES. He starts his routine with an imitation of his father telling him as a three year old, " Don't run in the house with a spoon in your mouth!" Then he says, "Good rule, Dad."

This little anecdote clearly shows that a three year old does not have the right to be wrong about running with a spoon in their mouth. Also, to carry the analogy forward, subordinates do not have the right to be wrong about everything. Opening up the decision-making process still requires a great deal of thought as to with which decisions one can live. Also, "the right to be wrong" is no new amendment to the employee Bill of Rights. This right must be clearly earned. It must also be developed since it will not just appear one day when you wake up. To reach this point, Phil Jackson said:

> "...I had to give the players the freedom to find out what worked and didn't. That meant putting them on the floor together in unusual combinations and letting them deal with treacherous situations without bailing them out."

This is a style of management called empowerment. When someone asked me what I wanted out of life, my answer was that I wanted my sons to grow up to be men. This leads to a parental style designed to empower at each stage of their development with decision-making responsibilities that do not have that active, guiding hand unless great harm can come from a disastrous decision. This is easier said than done. It takes restraint to allow mistakes. But this is a way for learning how to make decisions.

One of the most harmful parental and management styles around is what I call, "The do as I say, not as I do" philosophy. If you want your children not to smoke, you will do them no greater favor than to quit smoking. The more importance that you put to a rule, the more diligence you should have in following it yourself. Never forget that it is your job to lead and this means setting the example for your subordinates. This obvious statement is violated more times than you could possibly guess by those in power. General Patton noted,

> "When I was a second lieutenant I had a captain who was very sloppy and usually late, yet he got after the men for just those faults; he was a failure. The troops I have commanded have always been well dressed...because I have set the example in these qualities."

We have all seen the very people responsible for creating a dress code violate that code. The very people responsible for a smoke-free workplace violate the policy themselves. What does this say to your subordinates other than, "Do as I say, not as I do?" It also creates resentment and creates an atmosphere not conducive to respect. It separates you from your subordinates in destructive ways. Certainly there will be things that you have earned the right to do that your subordinates have not. The military has privilege of rank and corporations have perks. But even if you are an owner, you should take care in flaunting these differences. Make sure you understand which ones are truly rights you possess and not whims. The aim of being a good leader is respect. Acts that are viewed as capricious foster resentment, which is not a goal of parenting or management.

Respect is something you have to give in order to receive. In fact, the amount of respect that you get is proportional to the amount you dispense. The whole notion of respect is usually viewed from the negative, disrespect and insubordination from below. This frequently reveals that the leader does not treat subordinates with respect. Many managers believe respect is to be received in only one direction--from the bottom flowing up.

Too many managers want to change the world or their environment without changing themselves. They make rules for everybody else, but not themselves. The real key to successful management lies in the way in which you approach life. Everything else will follow suit if you act with respect, are loyal to your subordinates, and get organized yourself before organizing your department. In other words, approach your role as a manager in a Soulful manner.

Zen Master Shunryu Suzuki hints at an inward management style in his book, *Zen Mind, Beginner's Mind,*

> "When we have our body and mind in order, everything else will exist in the right place, in the right way. But usually, without being aware of it, we try to change something other than ourselves, we try to order things outside us. But it is impossible to organize things if you yourself are not in order. When you do things in the right way, at the right time, everything else will be organized."

In this book there have been quotes from coaches like Vince Lombardi, Pat Riley, Mike Ditka and Phil Jackson. Other quotes come from great teachers like Kip Thorne or military leaders like Patton. These great leaders would have succeeded in any chosen profession. Their strengths were many but at the top of the list has to be building a group awareness that took precedence over the individual. Phil Jackson said it best:

> "This is the struggle every leader faces: how to get members of the team who are driven by the quest for individual glory to give themselves over wholeheartedly to the group effort. In other words, how to teach them selflessness."

It is the job of every coach, manager, military leader or CEO to instill the idea that we are connected to each other in meaningful ways. The sense of oneness is a powerful understanding that makes the whole much greater than the sum of its parts. It makes your organization, be it family, team, department, or company, much more effective as a unit rather than a collection of individuals.

We have already spoken about how it is essential for management to develop a vision infused with Soul, how responsibility must flow from the heart of management, the importance of giving one's passion and energy freely, and the essence of marketing with Soul. These concepts are part of what it means to lead with Soul.

If there is one concept to distill what the best leaders, managers, entrepreneurs, teachers, scientists, or CEOs all possess, it is the ability to make connections among less than obvious events. Making connections between internal and external situations (Synchronicity), between attitudes and facts, and making connections between the corporation and the society at large is an ongoing process.

Leaders must supply the drive or energy to motivate those who follow. They must lead with more than technical competence. They should be not only technically qualified but have qualities of dignity, honor and decency. In short, they must exhibit the highest of standards. They must themselves have Soul.

Some ways in which leaders are selected are flat out wrong. As a child, usually the most prolific baseball player was chosen as the captain, regardless of any special aptitude for leading. Hitting a ball the farthest does not confer on a player any more extraordinary leadership talents than having 20:15 eyesight. A great salesperson does not always make a great sales manager. Being great in mathematics does not make one a great teacher.

With the above examples, I am not trying to say that merit has no place in the corporate environment. What I am saying is that great leadership skills lie outside the realm of simply looking at the technical capabilities required by each profession. Pat Riley, Phil Jackson, Vince Lombardi, Kip Thorne, and Tom Landry were all better leaders than they were players.

To be sure sometimes people are gifted with being great at both the practice of the craft and its teaching. Mike Ditka, George Patton and Niels Bohr come instantly to mind. In today's corporate environment, not enough emphasis is placed on the notion that a major responsibility of management is to train, teach, and make oneself obsolete. A worthwhile goal is to make oneself as if invisible.

A good leader sees connections that evade other people. They make connections between the actual resources at their disposal and the larger picture crafted from their vision. This involves placing people in the best possible position to succeed instead of forcing people into positions not best suited for their talents.

Once again, the Zen, basketball coach Phil Jackson said it well when he said,

> "Just as fish don't fly and elephants don't play rock and roll, you can't expect a team to perform that's out of tune with its basic abilities...In other words, you can dream all you want, but, bottom line, you've got to work with what you've got. Otherwise you're wasting your time...when your vision is based on a clear-sighted assessment of your resources, alchemy often mysteriously transforms into a force greater than the sum of its individual talents. Inevitably, paradoxically, the acceptance of boundaries and limits is the gateway to freedom."

How many times have you seen in an organization the imposition of tasks on people wholly unqualified? It is as if a manager discovers a need and looks around for the most available person to fill the void. Usually the most available person is available precisely because they have managed to maneuver into a position of not being busy.

I have been around organizations that had the most unlikely, ill-suited people doing tasks for which they were so obviously wrong. This was not their fault. It was management's responsibility for putting their personnel in positions to fail. In most cases the inevitable failure was deemed to be a defect, not in management, but in the misplaced individual. By not accepting the boundaries or limitations of individual talent, one is sure to get bad results. The same happens if you misjudge those limitations.

Judging the strengths and weaknesses of all of the resources at your disposal is critical to good leadership and management. It cannot be a jaundiced view that sees poor tools everywhere in the toolbox. Nor should the view originate from behind rose-colored glasses. Good management sees the value that every subordinate has, and it is up to the manager to liberate the talents that each person possesses.

A good leader recognizes that not everybody is an eagle but that each person doesn't need to remain earthbound. To carry the metaphor further, a good leader helps his flock to fly higher and higher as they develop. This is done with training, matching skills with talents, inspiration, and all the other reflections of Soul we have been outlining.

In the final analysis, good leaders blaze their own path on a journey of discovery. They also inspire those who wish to follow to seek their own path and to encourage that path even when it does not follow in their exact footsteps. Like a parent, they must encourage an independent path that leads to and from the same place: Soul.

Chapter Eight

Intuition

"...a holistic thinker...[is] constantly relying on hunches to cope with problems far too complex for rational analysis organizational effectiveness does not lie in that narrow minded concept called 'rationality;' it lies in a blend of clear logic and powerful intuition."

--Henry Mintzberg as quoted in the *Harvard Business Review*

"The fact of the matter is that, increasingly, policy makers are overwhelmed by events and information."

--Zbigniew Brzezinski, former National Security Advisor

"...powerful intuition cannot be rationally explained. It is not something teachable or reducible to rule, else we might all be geniuses. It wells up spontaneously from within."

--Banesh Hoffman, from the book *Albert Einstein: Creator and Rebel*

Who can deny that we live in a complex world? With information exploding at unprecedented rates, it is impossible for anyone to keep up with all the pertinent information in any particular field. Earlier we stated that information, and therefore knowledge, was doubling every three years. One of the byproducts of this phenomenon is that we are all too aware that we personally never have all of the available information to make perfectly reasoned decisions.

It is not the case that doctors, scientists, or businessmen previously had all the right information at their disposal. Frequently they may have had all of the *available* information because it was relatively easy to keep up in one's field of interest. With today's information explosion, this is no longer possible. We have become more acutely aware of the gaps in our knowledge and the limitations of our information. This awareness is one of the reasons for angst every time an important decision needs to be made. We have the sense that if we only had a little more time, a little more information, then we could go boldly into the future with our decisions. But limits for decision-making utilizing any body of knowledge must be recognized. Trammell Crow, once the country's biggest real estate developer summed up this problem well:

> "No man can retain in his consciousness all the things he knows and needs to make a decision. It's just too big a body of knowledge. I believe that business leaders take some positions and make some decisions transcendentally. Not magically. Intuitively."

So what are managers and executives to do with this overwhelming reality? Consult a Ouija board? Visit a fortune teller?

Or call a 900 psychic hotline for the real scoop? Nothing so corny is suggested by this chapter, although several leading businessmen in the past have done exactly the above. Cornelius Vanderbilt consulted clairvoyants regularly for business and personal advice. J.P. Morgan visited fortune tellers and H.L. Hunt picked oil properties with the help of a psychic. There is even a popular seminar in astrology for brokers hoping to chart the stock market in relation to the stars.

What this entire book proposes is letting Soul emerge in every phase of corporate endeavor. This is especially true in the decision-making process. This can be done utilizing values and intuition. Intuition is a word that is widely understood colloquially but has been marginalized by old paradigm thinking that placed exclusive worth on reason and rationality. An executive is not supposed to say, " I feel...," he is supposed to say, "I think..." Women say "I feel," and few executives want to be ripped away from the old boys' network and lumped in with a "female" way of expression.

Intuition is not a female quality at all. It is a human quality that in many ways is one of the qualities that makes us human. Intuition comes from the Latin word *intuori*, which means "to look in; to see with the mind's eye." We have all heard the echo of an inner voice instructing us on doing this or that. Sometimes intuition comes in visual flashes or as just mentioned as an inner voice. Physicist and writer Alan Lightman has said,

> "Scientists often make their greatest discoveries just at the moment when they follow their intuition instead of equations. In other words, when they behave the least 'Scientifically.'"

Sometimes the intuitive spark is called the "Aha! Experience" or the "Eureka Factor," but by any other name it is still intuition. Scientists and businessmen have been reluctant to break an informal code of silence (until they reach the pinnacle of their profession) by expounding how much intuition is relied upon in the act of creation or in making decisions. This is not the case when we speak to top athletes in football, basketball, and baseball.

Larry Bird has said that when his game was "on," he could *feel* where everybody was on the court. He said, "It's scary. When I'm at my best I can do just about anything I want and no one can stop me. I feel I'm in total control of everything." He was using intuition. It is no wonder it pained him to retire--what a feeling to be in the flow of life, in so perfect harmony that almost an altered state of consciousness was achieved.

Arguably, Michael Jordan is the greatest basketball player ever to have played the game. When he is "in a zone," he approaches the free-throw line and shoots *with his eyes closed*. This is similar to the way Zen Masters shoot arrows at targets with their eyes closed. Jordan sees with an inner eye. This is a form of intuition. John Brodie, the Hall of Fame quarterback and announcer said that the best athletes develop "an extraordinary state of mind" that makes decision-making effortless and below the level of consciousness.

Growing up in the Sixties I was privileged to watch Gale Sayers, the Hall of Fame halfback for the Chicago Bears. He was the most elusive runner of his day. When asked about how he knew where to juke and move, he simply said that he did not even *know* what he was going to do; he would just feel his way through the hole. The great ones, Ty Cobb, Rogers Hornsby,

Tony Gwynne, Willie Mays, Henry Aaron, Kareem Abdul Jabbar, and the Big O, Oscar Robertson, have stated the importance of intuition and catching the flow or feel of the game to be successful. What they were all speaking about was intuition.

But intuitive abilities far exceed the playing fields or courts of athletics. These intuitive abilities have been documented in our corporate environment for years. This is a book about Soul in the workplace and what it will take to be an effective manager or CEO in the next millennium. I am a firm believer that people who reach the pinnacle of their professions have something to offer everyone if we engage in listening with proper attention. The athletes above are telling us something profound and they are secure enough to share some of their secrets of success.

In the business world, we are fortunate to have many fine examples of how the inner voice, "the gut feeling," proved to be the decisive element in the decision-making process. Robert Jensen, CEO of General Cable Corporation, was once quoted in *Fortune* magazine concerning his multi-million dollar investment decision-making process, "On each decision, the mathematical analysis only got me to the point where my intuition had to take over."

Ray Kroc of McDonald's was cautioned by all of his lawyers and everybody else not to purchase the chain that he had at that time built up to 228 restaurants. The price tag, he was told, was exorbitant: $2.7 million. It was more than it was worth at the time. Later he would recall, "I'm not a gambler and I didn't have that kind of money, but *my funnybone instinct* kept urging me on. So I closed my office door, cussed up and down, and threw things out the window. Then I called the lawyer back and said, 'Take it!'"

Obviously his "funnybone instinct" refers to intuition. In hindsight, intuitive genius almost always seems obvious. Looking from today's vantage point, Ray Kroc paying "too much" for the chain seems silly. But had he listened to reason and his advisors, the landscape of America may have been less tens of thousands of arches.

It may seem unsettling at first to encourage intuition within an organization. We do not understand how this beguiling process works and just like everything else in the world, we do not all have the same intuitive abilities any more than we have the same abilities to dunk a basketball. We will address this a bit later. But the best leaders and teachers do encourage intuition among their troops. The "master" physics instructor, Kip Thorne at Cal Tech recognized the role of intuition and encouraging creativity by,

> "...cloistering his half a dozen students within adjacent rooms with an unwritten rule that office and lab doors remain open. Someone, in a group of creative people working together, is usually quivering at the edge of discovery, and vibrations spread."

This works in the corporate environment as well. It takes a different kind of leadership to encourage this kind of openness and energy. Intuitive people always seem to be quivering at the edge of discovery and Professor Thorne believed it was transferable.

Without making this a treatise on consciousness, it may help to ask the question "From where does intuition spring?" The answer is both simple and complex. It comes from inside. It is what one practitioner called "the vapor of past experience." It springs from the depth of our psyche or Soul. It is almost as if we hear a faint whisper or echo from "another" guiding our thoughts. At levels deep within our psyche there is a connection to what Carl Jung called, "the collective unconscious." It is from here that we hear the whispers, echoes, see shadows and reflections of a shared reality with the totality of Mankind.

Jung said, "individual consciousness is based on and surrounded by an *indefinitely extended unconscious type*." Individual consciousness is linked to a collective mind that lies below the level of our personal, conscious awareness. The connection between our personal consciousness and this "collective mind" may be an explanation for intuition. Psychiatrist June Singer further developed this link between an individual psychology and collective unconscious which she believes is the source of new ideas or intuition:

"...Each person's consciousness emerges like an island from the great sea in which all find their base, with the rim of wet sand encircling each island corresponding to the 'personal conscious.' But it is the collective unconscious--that sea--that is the birthplace of all consciousness, and from there the old ideas arise anew, and their connections with contemporary situations are initiated."

This collective mind or unconscious has also been called the "Soul." Could it be that intuition is the expression of Soul advancing into personal awareness? Intuitive people have trained their ears to listen to these faint and often fleeting messages from the collective "pool." It is as if intuitive flashes come from external sources yet are part of us. This paradox disappears when the relationship between personal and collective worlds are understood. The relationship demystifies intuition by placing Soul as the communicator. For intuition to flourish, we must open the communication channels--to let the Soul speak. We cannot force Soul to speak on demand.

One of the most intuitive scientists was Albert Einstein. His biographer, Banesh Hoffman commented on Einstein's anxiety about the possible limits and source of intuition:

> "Einstein had misgivings, likening himself to a hen that is expected to lay eggs and wondering whether he would be able to produce further ideas on demand--as he put it years later in a different connection: 'ideas from God.'"

Intuitive insights cannot be demanded or reduced to demands of reason. They are a spiritual gift from the Soul, or if one is religiously inclined, from God. Einstein biographer, Hoffman continues:

> "Yet when we see how shaky were the ostensible foundations on which Einstein built his theory [General Theory of Relativity], we can only marvel at the intuition that guided him to his masterpiece. Such intuition is the essence of genius...By a sort of *divination,* genius knows from the start in a nebulous way the goal toward which it must strive. The painful journey through uncharted country it bolsters its confidence by plausible arguments...These arguments do not have to be sound so long as they serve the irrational, clairvoyant, subconscious drive that is really in command. Indeed we should not expect them to be sound in a sterile, logical sense..."

Here Hoffman, a scientist himself, understands that intuition seems divinely inspired. It is as if the answers exist and it is through intuition that we can discover them. This is not subject to sterile logic or reason. Intuition may be bolstered by reason (plausible arguments), but an internal communication mechanism with the collective unconscious lies outside this process. This is why discussions of intuition must of necessity be discussions of Soul.

When intuition is used properly, it serves as a link between the Soul and events. It is an expression of harmony between the self and external events. This harmony is expressed as a "feeling." It is certainly a guiding impulse that should always be taken into consideration. This will be discussed in greater detail in the next chapter on *Synchronicity*.

Before we move any further, and some of you readers think we are headed for metaphysical nonsense, I am not suggesting that we chuck reason out the door and solely rely on a vague notion or feeling. We are endowed with considerable faculties of reason. We should always employ all of our abilities when faced with tough decisions. Reason **and** intuition should be marshaled in pursuit of corporate objectives. In tandem, they form a team that can be used to check and validate the other. Unfortunately, intuitive insights all too often fail to weather the storms of reason. Roy Rowan in *The Intuitive Manager* wrote:

> "...an ingenious new idea that doesn't survive a logical assault isn't necessarily wrong. When Robert Goddard suggested rocket propulsion as the only feasible power source for space travel, critics quite logically, it seemed, scorned the idea, insisting there isn't anything in space for the rocket to push against. But rockets, we know now, work because the momentum of the hot gases rushing backward is matched by the forward momentum of the rocket's shell."

Reason should be used in concert with intuition but not as an assault weapon. Reason and intuition should counsel decision-making, not control the process. Achieving balance between these different types of counsel is a worthwhile goal. Jonas Salk, the discoverer of the polio vaccine, wrote a book entitled the *Anatomy of Reality: Merging of Intuition and Reason*. In the book he lays out the need to balance inspiration and logic:

> "A new way of thinking is now needed to deal with our present reality. Our subjective responses (intuitional) are more sensitive and more rapid than our objective responses (reasoned). This is the nature of the way the mind works. We first sense and then we reason why...intuition must be allowed a free reign and be allowed to play."

Many people and disciplines have called the above dichotomy by many names; Left brain/Right brain, Feminine/Masculine, or Yin and Yang. The point here is to recognize that there is more than one way to look at reality. If we want to make the most enlightened decisions it would be helpful to synthesize or balance these opposites. Our complex world demands a balanced approach. This means that we must not flip back and forth between opposite poles. We must learn to transcend the bipolar way of viewing reality.

Intuition is not necessarily mystical. We all have a sense of what it is yet as soon as we try to grasp it with all of our reason...it seems to evaporate. But whether you believe that intuition is no more than reason applied by our subconscious or an expression of a knowledge stemming from absolute consciousness within, we cannot deny the phenomenon. It most certainly exists. My personal sense is that it cannot be grasped by reason. It must be grasped by experience.

Having said all of the above, I want to reiterate that reason should never be abandoned. Intuition should, as much as possible, be subjected to thorough analysis. The act of articulating and defending intuitive insights is a good exercise. Sometimes a brilliant intuitive insight is beyond articulation, but one should always attempt to critically assess intuition. On the other hand, courses of action derived from a quantitative, rational process should also be subjected to the intuitive critique. How does a decision "feel?" What does your gut tell you?

The most successful businesspeople have learned to synthesize these two qualities. Our intuitive abilities have become buried under the weight of 300 years of scientific rationality and reductionist scientism. Intuition leads us from the hard edge of a materialistic, mechanistic world-view and aids us in navigating the spiritual flow of an organic, new paradigm world-view. Every human possesses vestigial intuitive abilities; they are part of our very being. Intuition is an expression of Soul speaking to us and if we learn to accept the validity of its expression, then our personal and professional lives will be enriched.

If you have read this far and have played back in your mind all the times you didn't listen to your intuition, you may be thinking that you will begin to trust your gut a bit more in the future. If you are a manager or CEO, you are not just dealing with your own intuition, but everyone else's gut feelings as well. It is quite one thing to trust your own feelings, but how are you going to trust someone else's gut?

It has happened to me more times than I can count. Each and every time someone in my company told me that they wanted to do something out of the ordinary because they "had a feeling," my first knee-jerk reaction was a different kind of feeling...a feeling of, "uh oh!" This was, after all, somebody else's gut that I was being asked to follow. If following your own intuition is hard, wait until you are faced with someone else's gut as the source of inspiration for a particular course.

I will not cop out and say that I relied on my own gut to tell me when to follow someone else's intuition. As a manager you have to learn to judge abilities all of the time. Judging someone's intuitive skills must be judged as well. You do this by communicating more so you know the basis for a suggestion and allowing certain decisions, small at first, to be made by subordinates who claim intuition. You take note of the results.

You want to encourage honesty from subordinates and not force rationalizations. Intuition has such a bad rap in many companies because if someone has an intuitive insight, they cloak the insight in such strained language that they often marginalize themselves before long. We said earlier that intuition should be subjected to critical analysis, but keep in mind that the goal is to foster discourse. Seeking to stimulate insight and not dampen the spirit should also be part of the critique process.

Everybody has different levels of skill with all endeavors, and intuition is no different. You will eventually know which subordinates' intuitive decisions you can trust and which ones substitute a form of bad guessing for true intuitive insight. Remember that intuition is not a guess--it is an insight.

This chapter is not dedicated to instructing you on developing intuition in yourself or your subordinates. (For further treatment of this subject we have reviewed a few books on this topic at the end of this book.) It would be nice if we could list 10 simple steps for increasing your intuitive capacity. The aim here is to make the case for allowing intuition to enter into your business world...to take it out of the closet.

In the final analysis, it is the dance between reason and this other kind of knowledge that must be learned. Synthesizing these often antagonistic forces is what is needed to cope with our modern-day corporate environment. Unfortunately there is no single process that we can follow. All roads may lead to Rome, but there are an infinite number of roads to get us there. The road for each one of us is filled with deep potholes that we must navigate around, but the journey itself is rewarding for yourself as well as your organization.

Chapter Nine
Synchronicity

"In writing this paper I have, so to speak, made good a promise which for many years I lacked the courage to fulfill. [I have] attempt[ed] to broach a problem in such a way as to reveal some of its manifold aspects and connections and to open up a very obscure field. In most cases they were things which people do not talk about for fear of exposing themselves to thoughtless ridicule. I was amazed to see how many people have had experiences of this kind and how carefully the secret was guarded. So my interest in this problem has a human as well as a scientific foundation."

--C. G. Jung, from the forward in *Synchronicity*

"Chance favors the prepared mind."
--Proverb

With the above words, C.G. Jung, one of the greatest psychiatrists of all time, took a bold step in attempting to describe the phenomenon of how the universe and psyche were linked together in an almost mystical manner. The reader has followed me this far and admittedly, this is a speculative chapter. I will state flat out that this chapter may not be for everyone. My hope is that whatever truths may preside in the previous chapters will stand on their own. In attempting to explain the role synchronicity plays in human and corporate affairs, I have tried to bring an obscure field to a new audience.

It is first necessary to come to a general understanding of what synchronicity is. Simply put, synchronicity is the phenomenon that meaningfully connects seemingly random events when there is no logical cause between or among those events. The connections lie outside the laws of cause and effect. These events can be either internal (psychological thoughts or feelings) or external (meaning events happening around us.) We have all had that eerie feeling that meaningful coincidences occur in clusters that are linked together but have no causal explanation. It may be you have been thinking about a friend whom you have not seen for years and the phone rings and it is that friend. Synchronistic events can connect us to something profound within ourselves, family or business. It leads us to our Soul if we become aware of the experiences.

Jung wrote about an incident between a patient and himself,

> "A young woman I was treating had, at a critical moment, a dream in which she was given a golden scarab. While she was telling me this dream I sat with my back to the closed window. Suddenly I hear a noise behind me, like a gentle tapping. I turned around and

saw a flying insect knocking against the windowpane
from outside. I opened the window and caught the creature in the air as it flew in. It was the nearest analogy to
a golden scarab that one finds in our latitudes, a
scarabaeid   beetle,   the   common   rose-chafer
(*Cetoniaaurata*), which contrary to its usual habits, had
evidently felt an urge to get into a dark room at this particular moment."

The above example was a meaningful coincidence that eventually helped Jung treat his patient. For the patient, this event was
so significant that it broke her excessive dependence on reason
and rationality. The event led to her accepting things outside
reason. This was one of her problems, a disconnection from the
spiritual side of her nature. The event suggests a connection
between the patient's inner psychic realm (her dream) and
external, actual events. This is synchronicity. The
Synchronicity Principle postulates that there exists an order to
the Universe and that it is for us to discover the interconnec-
tions of that order.

Many cultures readily accept the idea of synchronicity and
have developed elaborate systems to discover the harmony and
order of the Universe that lies outside known natural laws. The
Chinese have *I Ching*. This is a method of casting sticks
(yarrow stalks) or coins. A picture (hexagram) is drawn and
then interpreted. There are 64 hexagrams that describe the
nature of the Universe. They believe that at any point in time,
the Universe represents itself in a microcosm through the different combinations and patterns created by the hexagrams
drawn from the "throws."

As hard as it appears to the Western, rational mind, this method has been used for thousands of years. The Chinese do not believe that the sticks **cause** events to unfold; they merely indicate a link between the thrower and the Universe. When I was growing up, my parents had sent my two sisters and me to Palestine to live with my grandparents for a year to learn about our culture. My uncle and his wife also lived in the house. She was an older lady who the village thought had special abilities. She never went to school and could neither read nor write. Her particular ability was to "read" patterns left when emptied coffee cups were turned upside down.

If you ever drank Turkish Coffee (we called it Arabian Coffee), you would notice a thick, muddy residue left over at the bottom of the demitasse. If you turn the cup over after the coffee is emptied and let it set for a couple of minutes, a pattern or matrix forms on the inside of the cup that has many branch-like figures. They look almost like lines created in a glass ant colony. Her "reading" was for each person who drank the coffee. Each pattern was different. Like the hexagrams created from casting yarrow sticks, the patterns were thought to represent a particular person's relationship to the Universe at that particular moment. Leaving aside the fact that her readings were uncannily accurate, the point is that there are hundreds of millions of people that already believe that the Universe represents itself in a microcosm and it is up to us to "tune in" to the way reality is represented.

Two recent synchronistic events may help clarify the connection between internal and external events. I was hiking up one of the trails of Squaw Peak in Phoenix, Arizona. When I reached the top, I decided to sit on a rock to meditate. I had been under the stress of a very big business deal and had several reservations as to how I should approach it. About halfway into the meditation, a violent thought erupted in my mind, and anger, not to mention a few choice vulgarities, began to surge right through me.

Before I could get back to the quiet of meditation, I heard a loud hissing sound. I looked back and there was a ten-inch, dark gray lizard perched on a rock about two feet behind my left shoulder. I was startled but moved ever so close so that my face was about 12 inches from the lizard. The lizard did not move, but its eye closest to me opened and followed my movement. It stayed still although it is a frequent habit of this animal to be easily startled.

It was as if this primordial creature was responding to my anger by appearing and signaling to my consciousness the idea of counterproductive anger. My anger did not cause the lizard to appear. This was a meaningful coincidence that actually helped me overcome my anger. This was a synchronistic event.

The flip side of nature reflecting a negative emotion occurred a few days later when I was attending an outside concert. I chanced upon a superb local reggae band that had the crowd delighted in their island beat. I noticed in the crowd a girl with Down's Syndrome who was swaying to the music so perfectly in beat. She had attracted a great deal of attention because her joy was so apparent and pure; it was infectious.

I remember a wave of joy filling me. I was sitting on the grass without shoes and socks when I noticed this butterfly landing on my toe. For 20 minutes I looked at this same butterfly leave my foot, fly around, and then land on either my shoulder or toe.

It never landed on another person. It was as if it became my partner in the moment of bliss and joy I was experiencing. This was a connection between my internal feeling and external events--hence synchronicity.

The idea that the Universe represents itself on many levels may seem odd. The first time that I had become acquainted with fractals and chaos theory, I was overwhelmed. I am not a mathematician so the concepts were vague to me. But the idea that there are certain patterns in nature that reoccur was equally astonishing. After viewing aerial pictures of a coastline that had a particular shape and seeing another photo of a cove within that coastline with the same shape, the patterns of nature began to have a different meaning for me. It opened up the possibility that there is order to the Universe that at times requires a different perspective for awareness to surface.

What we have come to understand is that we live in a unitary Universe. All of the great religions have taught us this and now our science has begun teaching these same lessons. Zen Masters have said you can look into infinity by looking inside. Famous warrior and Native American spiritual leader Black Elk wrote in *The Sacred Pipe*, "Peace comes within the Souls of men when they realize their relationship, their oneness with the universe and all its powers, and when they realize that at the center of the Universe dwells the Great Spirit, and that this center is really everywhere. It is within each of us." This is one of the great lessons in Chief Seattle's letter to the President reprinted at the beginning of "Responsibility and Soul."

We can tap into this power and knowledge if we can get to the point of perceiving reality in a new way. What we need is a new perspective to understand reality. If we take the leap and say that our own psyche is in a way a microcosm of the Universe, then we can more fully examine the connections with our heart and Soul. This means that within us resides the wisdom and knowledge to navigate the difficult waters of life. We need only to see and hear from this new perspective to discover what actions are appropriate.

So what do the above musings have to do with being a manager or CEO of a corporation? If our reality is shaped by the way we perceive it and if our external conditions are represented by our internal world, we have an additional set of tools to use in managing our affairs. This perspective validates the role of intuition in decision-making. It also gives credence to the phenomenon of positive thinking. If external events and internal thoughts are related, we can understand why so many good things happen to positive people. William James, the famous psychologist, said, "Our *belief* at the beginning of a doubtful undertaking is the one thing that ensures the successful outcome of your venture."

The postulation of Synchronicity as an explanation of positive thinking should not be interpreted as "positive thinking **causes** positive external results." Norman Vincent Peale might have thought that, but Jung did not. Synchronicity lies outside the causal realm. It is a reflection of the ordered Universe. If good things happen to positive thinkers, they are a reflection that the thinker is in harmony with the Universe.

As a manager or businessperson, you are faced with many alternatives and decisions to make. When you are gripped by an unshakable belief, a belief that emanates from the depths of your Soul, then it is likely that this belief is also a reflection of the ordered Universe. That is what, "ensures the successful outcome of your venture."

This suggests that the way in which a manager, coach, or CEO can find the right course of action is to look inward until one develops a belief that is in harmony with external events. Once a belief springs from the depths of the Soul, rather than imposed by wishful thinking, it must of necessity reflect the larger world. Success is ensured once harmony is achieved.

A very significant premise of *Corporate Soul* is that we must find ways to become consciously aware of the connections that already exist between our internal Soul and our external actions. Imposing a thought into our minds and endlessly repeating that thought will not create an external world in the image of that thought. Synchronicity suggests a theoretical framework for explaining our reality. If synchronicity as a principle or theory is valid, then the answers to all the problems we possess lie within our own Soul.

The corporate world spends so much time trying to impose its will on Nature that so little time is spent attempting to understand the harmonic dance and subtle answers to all of our problems that are revealed through synchronistic events. A few examples may help demystify this topic. We can get a glimpse at seeing a hidden order in events that lie outside causation and outside reason. The following example has happened to everyone at one time or another.

Have you ever known a person who was getting into a series of car accidents time after time? If you would check, I bet you dollars to navy beans that there was internal psychic turmoil going on in that person's life. The psychological turmoil is a reflection from a subconscious level of the physical world of events. The external events and internal events are mutual reflections and a window into each other's world. Accidents should in fact be a wake up call to right your psychic ship. It is as if the Universe communicates with us all the time to bring things to consciousness to give us an additional perspective. We need to turn our attention to the signs. This is synchronicity.

We have all heard that "Necessity is the Mother of invention." But what does this really mean? It seems true enough that answers to our problems mysteriously emerge out of the awareness of necessity. Synchronicity is one theory to explain this phenomenon. Psychiatrist Jean Bolden has described this process in *The Tao of Psychology*,

> "Whatever I need to become more conscious of, whatever could be an Achilles heel, whatever is my growing edge, synchronistically seems to arrive on my doorstep. Realizing this, when synchronicity seems to be playing a hand in bringing someone to me, I now wonder whether it will be a meeting of special significance for me as well as for the patient."

The Chinese have an ancient saying, "When the pupil is ready, the teacher will come." The above quote from Dr. Bolden and the Chinese proverb describe a twist on the American proverb, " Necessity is the Mother of invention." It is also the case that as the intensity of a problem escalates, being personal or business in nature, we become more receptive to ideas that reveal themselves to us. Answers to our problems exist all around us; they manifest themselves in many forms. Synchronicity is the process that once understood can help us grasp meaning from an ordered Universe. Many people believe that there exists a matrix of intersecting realities. The following illustration of this matrix is an example of how synchronicity can affect the business. It is the story of the publication of *Jonathan Livingston Seagull* as told by Roy Rowan:

> "Eleanor Friede, the book's publisher, uses...the word "matrix" to describe the confluence of forces she believes entered into the success of [the book]. First, following a *chance* meeting with Bach [the author], she salvaged the manuscript that two dozen publishers had already turned down. Then, as she explains, 'the accompanying illustrations submitted by Bach were paintings of birds that looked as if they were stuffed.' Macmillan wouldn't consider the expense of assigning a photographer. *But by chance*, photographer Russell Munson, an old friend of Bach's, had many years earlier won a special grant to photograph seagulls. He had an old box of negatives stashed away in his studio, where Bach slept when he came to New York...But what really convinces her now that this slender volume had some extra, inexplicable impetus behind it was the mystical power it seemed to exert over its readers."

Here we see that there are a series of coincidences that are linked in an acausal (without cause) chain. The book's editor had her mind prepared for these "chance" occurrences, and the result was a resounding success in book publishing.

The frontiers of modern physics, biology, mathematics, and chemistry have identified a "self-organizing" principle that creates order out of complex, chaotic systems. We do not know why patterns in nature continually reoccur, but the wonder is that they *do*. The Synchronicity Principle seems to explain how these patterns are connected. If we believe in the significance of these patterns and connections, then we must become mindful of them to help guide our actions in a complex world.

As a corporate manager, entrepreneur, or CEO, you must learn to read or tune in to the signs that come from internal sources as well as synchronistic external events. They both are ways in which the Universe is speaking to us. Learning this process is a lifelong task. It is certainly one of the joys of living. Learning to be receptive to unfolding events can be a spiritual quest as well as an enormous benefit to your organization.

We have to understand that our Soul speaks to us in many ways. As mentioned earlier it may be a faint echo or vision. Our Soul speaking to us may represent itself in more dramatic ways that include neuroses and even psychoses. Even these drastic disorders may prove beneficial when we become aware of them and can actually lead us to create balance in our lives when properly understood. The mystery of life is to discover purpose in what the Soul has to say. It is one of the wonders of life that we possess these self-correcting psychological mechanisms. It is for us to listen to our Soul.

Intuition and synchronicity are related insofar as synchronicity helps shed light on this internal communication process. Remember synchronicity assumes an ordered Universe in which patterns can be represented in a microcosm. When intuition bubbles up from within, it is our Soul speaking to us. It is meaningful communication and corresponds to external events.

Synchronistic events, when understood, lead to reevaluating decisions and policies. Unplanned consequences of one's business decisions can be seen in a new light, and many have hidden meaning when a different eye is turned toward them. We can learn what to do by examining what is in our own heart and mind because we hold all the answers within. This is where as Chinese Master Lao Tsu said lies, "...the gate to all mystery."

It is very difficult to control Nature. Synchronicity allows for a way to tap into the flow of our reality. If you do not believe that we live in a random Universe and see the harmony and exquisite order present, then we must attempt to align ourselves with that order. We hold the key to destiny in our own hands by walking through that mysterious gate. Understanding synchronicity as a process and force of Nature allows us to transform ourselves and therefore our reality. Dr. Bolden wrote,

> "Synchronistic meetings are like mirrors, reflecting back to us something of ourselves. In order to grow, we should take a good look. Synchronicity holds the promise that if we change from within, the patterns in our outer life will change also. If the people and events are here because we have drawn them here, then what happens in our lives apparently by chance or fortune is not really accidental."

If we want to change our lives then we must begin by reconnecting with the order of Nature. Brute willpower to overcome realities can be frustrating and counterproductive. I can personally vouch for this as my head is still sore from attempting to knock down brick walls by running into them without a helmet. In the past my approach to a problem meant applying as much willpower and energy I could muster to the situation. Whether successful or not, the ordeal always left me exhausted.

Believing that the Universe has order and contains a blueprint that unfolds does not mean we are passive in the unfolding. Remember we are part of this Universe. As Carl Sagan says, "We are all made up of star stuff." We have the power to discern this blueprint and to be an active participant in the unfolding. We must synthesize the duality between an ordered Universe and our free will to participate and create our world. In many ways, understanding synchronicity frees us from the whims of chance. It suggests that we can create our own luck or chance, by better preparing our minds and by seeking harmony. This is liberating in itself!

I have tried to present the concept of synchronicity in the hopes that by doing so, the way might be prepared for the uninitiated to further delve into this theory. To understand the harmony between the inner and external world cannot be captured by words alone--it must be experienced. This experiential knowledge lies outside reason, outside discourse.

Someone once told me that you could not describe the experience (flavor) of vanilla to anyone who had never already experienced the vanilla flavor. Once a shared frame of reference existed, then and only then could a conversation be intelligible. Still, though, you can never be sure if each of your experiences of "vanillaness" is the same. We each experience things in a unique manner.

I have also tried to share with you some of my own experiences. As a businessman who has traveled all over the world and started my career as a completely quantitative, logic-driven reductionist and mechanistic thinker, I know that this way of relating to your organization, family, and in general the environment, must change to survive the challenges ahead.

In the final analysis we must acknowledge the value of Soul in our personal and corporate lives. We must gather our resources and nourish the seeds planted in our midst. We have our destiny in our own hands, and as corporate executives we must also note that we have responsibilities far exceeding our own idiosyncratic world.

Business is a sacred enterprise. We who have chosen the path of entrepreneur, manager, or corporate executive need to reconnect spirituality with our path. We cannot stick our heads into the sand and take a narrow view of our enterprise. It is time for us to assume leadership in transforming society by discovering and creating harmony. We must believe in the notion that we are all members in the family of Man.

Chapter Ten
Secret of Victory

by George S. Patton, Jr.
With commentary by Jaffer Ali

What follows is one of the most significant treatises on business and success that you are ever likely to read. Of course it was not written with this in mind. Patton meant to outline his philosophy for becoming victorious on the battlefield. Once upon a time it was in vogue in business schools to read *The Art of War* by Sun Tzu and now it is time to learn from another warrior, General George S. Patton, Jr.

Those who are only familiar with Patton from George C. Scott's brilliant portrayal in the 1969 feature film are in for a treat. Patton was much more than a warrior, although he epitomized what a warrior was and remains to be. He was a poet, philosopher, classicist, and historian. He was a Renaissance man in a field not usually known for embracing notions of reincarnation (in which Patton ardently believed) or for allowing discussions of Soul to permeate one's discourse.

The following liberal excerpts from his essay are reprinted from Patton's personal papers. It was written March 26, 1926, when he was a Major. He had not yet achieved the fame that was to be his in WWII. His references to The World War refer to WWI. The perceptive reader will immediately see the analogies between many facets of *Corporate Soul* discussed throughout this book.

I have interjected commentary throughout. Patton's words are in boldface type and my own words follow in regular font. Patton's prose has a poetic quality so the reader may first want to read all of the excerpts first and then indulge in the commentary. For clarity of purpose, I have taken license to edit his essay and italicize certain parts of his phrases that are of special relevance to the topic of this book. It is with profound hope that we all can learn about creating a successful organization as well as living a victorious life by listening to what this marvel philosopher/warrior has to say.

Despite the years of thought and oceans of ink which have been devoted to the elucidation of war, its secrets still remain shrouded in mystery. War is an art and as such is not susceptible of *explanation to fixed formulae*. Yet, from the earliest times there has been an unending effort to subject its complex and emotional structure to dissection, to enunciate rules for its waging, to make tangible its intangibility. One might as well strive to isolate the Soul by dissection of the cadaver as to seek the essence of war by the analysis of its records.

Yet, the impossibility of physically detecting the Soul, its existence is proven by its tangible reflection in acts and thoughts.

Patton is a New Paradigm thinker who does not believe that we can reduce reality to formulas. When we dissect reality, we lose the intangible, human characteristics of Soul. He further believes that we come to know Soul by indirect means, its reflections in acts and thoughts. This is common to synchronistic events.

So with war, beyond its physical aspect of armed hosts there hovers an impalpable something which on occasion so dominates the material as to induce victory under circumstances quite inexplicable.

To understand this 'something,' we should seek it in a manner analogous to our search for the Soul; **and so seeking we shall perchance find it in the reflexes produced by the 'Great Captains.'**

Patton is not a philosophical materialist. He believes that "something" animates material, and this something is what we have been calling Soul. When the Soul dominates, victory inexplicably comes. He further suggests that we can learn the secrets of success from past great warriors since it is in the reflection of greatness that we come to know it.

But whither shall we turn for knowledge of their very selves? Not in the musty tomes of voluminous reports or censored recollections...nor yet in the countless histories where lesser wormish men have sought to snare their parted ghosts.

The great warriors were too busy and often too inept to write contemporaneously of their exploits. While what they later put on paper as biographies were retrospects colored by their vain strivings for enhanced fame...*War was an ebullition of their perished past.* The violent simplicity in execu-

**tion which procured success for them and which enthralled
the world looked pale and uninspired on paper; so they sea-
soned it...**

In order to understand the secret behind success, Patton challenges the way in which we get our information. Although Patton
was a military historian, he had little use for historians. He
thought of them like wormish business consultants. They could
only write about greatness, not experience it. Great warriors are
like great business men. Many do not write about what made
them great because they are too busy *being* great. Those who
write about themselves often appear as if their PR departments
wrote their biographies in their name. How can they capture the
ebullition, which means overwhelming passion, of "their perished past?" They cannot! So often those giants fail to write
about their greatness or make up things that sound good.

**So with the soldier. To pander to self-love and [human] urge
he attributes to his acts profound thoughts which never
existed.**

*The white hot energy of youth, which saw in obstacles but
inspirations, and in the enemy but the gage to battle*, **becomes
too complacent with age. The result of mathematical calcu-
lation and metaphysical erudition; of knowledge he never
had and plans he never made.**

**With the efforts of the historians, the case is even worse...no
matter when he writes, is by nature a man of thoughtful
and studious habits utterly incapable of appreciating the
roaring energy of a soldier...Colored by self-deception,
shaded by scholarly bookworms, our soldiers stand before**

us as devoid of life as the toothless portraits of Washington which adorn the walls of half our schoolrooms...

Patton is cautioning against relying upon soldiers' recollections as well as historians. We cannot apprehend the secret to victory with this often faulty information. A soldier's diary written years after the battle does not capture the "white-hot energy" nor does it capture the inspiration or passion of the effort. Historians do no better in capturing the spirit of the soldier.

Seeking obvious reasons for the obscure, we analyze their [warriors'] conduct as told by historians and assign as reasons for their success, apparent, trivial things.

Disregarding wholly the personality of Frederick, we attribute his victories to a tactical expedient, the oblique order of battle...Yet through the murk of fact and fable rises ever to our view this truth; 'The history of war is the history of warriors; few in number, mighty in influence.'

Alexander, not Macedonia, conquered the world. Scipio, not Rome, destroyed Carthage. Marlborough, not the Allies, defeated France. Cromwell, not the Roundheads, dethroned Charles.

Were this true only of warriors we might well exclaim, 'Behold the work of the historian,' *but it is equally the case in every human endeavor. Music has its myriad musicians, but only its dozen masters. So with painting, sculpture, literature, medicine, or trade. 'Many are called, but few are chosen.'*

Patton betrays the position of his class here. He was born into wealth and privilege. He believes that understanding greatness lies in studying great people. Understanding personality, which Patton uses interchangeably with Soul, is the way to great-ness...victory. Through the murk of trivial facts and exaggera-tions of fabled actions, the truth shines through. In every human endeavor, including business, we must get to know the masters. Are masters born?

Nor can we concur wholly with the alluring stories in the advertising sections of our magazines which point the gold-en path of success to all and sundry who will follow that particular phase of 'home education' that they happen to advocate. "Knowledge is power,' *but to a degree only. Its possession per se will raise a man to mediocrity, but not to dis-tinction. In our opinion, indeed, the instruction obtained from such courses is of less moment to future success than is the ambition which prompted the study.*

In considering these matters, sight should not be lost of the fact...there is much similarity...between the successful sol-dier and the successful man in other professions. Success due to knowledge and personality is the measure of ability in each case; but...with the soldier, success or failure means infinitely more as it must of necessity be measured not in terms of personal honor or affluence, but in life, happiness and honor of his men--his country.

Hence, the search for that elusive secret of military success; Soul, genius, personality--call it what you will--is of vital interest to us all.

Knowledge itself is important but not sufficient to master a pro-fession. At least its acquisition can lift a person to mediocrity, but not to the genius (master) level. Ambition in the individual is more important than obtaining information. This springs from inside and cannot be learned. Information without ambition is sterile. It must be infused with Soul for greatness.

One of the premises of this book is that we need different criteria for success rather than personal honor or wealth. Should not success be defined in terms of life, happiness, and honor of an entire organization...even country...world? A Soulful organization judges its success using the same criteria Patton used for military success. Soul is of "vital interest to us all," and it is truly the elusive secret of corporate, military and life's success.

...A British writer has said, 'The characteristic of war is its constant change of characteristic,' but as ever the case with aphorisms his remark needs explanation.

There is an incessant and constant change of 'means' to attain the inevitable 'end,' but we must take care not to let these inevitable sundry means, past or predicted, attain undue eminence in the perspective of our minds. *Since the beginning, there has been an unending cycle of them, and for each, its advocates have claimed adoption as the sole means of successful war.* **Yet, the records of all time show that the unchanging ends have been, are, and probably shall ever be, the securing of predominating force, of the right sort, at the right time.**

In seeking a premise for the enunciation of the rules for the employment of this predominating force, we must cull from past experience, or study, the most permanent characteristics, select our weapons, and assign to them that importance which reason and the analogy of experience indicate that they will attain.

Bearing these considerations, and the definition of predominant force, in mind, we shall resume our search for the secret of victory.

No matter what the situation, as to clarify of his mental perspective, the conscientious soldier approaches the solution of his problem more or less bemuddled by the phantoms of the past and deluded by unfounded or unproven hopes for the future...

Patton begins his own dissection of what it takes to achieve success. We need to examine the means we use to reach our goals but stop short of believing that the same methods will work in every situation. We are reminded here of business panaceas that are touted by various consulting "gurus" who apply one method for all corporate ends. These go in and out of fashion. There is TQM, Just In Time inventory management, reengineering, etc. Victory and success cannot be reduced to a formula given to us from a book or consultant.

In this scholarly avocation, soldiers of all important nations use at the present moment [a] method [that] not only familiarizes the student with all of the tools and technicalities of his trade, but also develops the aptitude for reaching decisions and the self-assurance derived from demonstrated achievements.

But as always, there is a fly in the ointment. *High academic performance demands infinite intimate knowledge of details, and the qualities requisite to such attainments often inhabit bodies lacking in personality.* Also the striving for such knowledge often engenders the fallacious notion that capac-

ity depends on the power to acquire such details, not the ability to apply them.

Obsessed with this thought, students...perish in a morass of knowledge where they first browsed for sustenance.

Patton is not against attaining knowledge. This is an important attribute of success. He believes that it is essential to learn the technical aspects of one's trade. But he is quick to note the limits of knowledge and the limits of the quest for knowledge has in attaining victory. Often those people with the most knowledge are those who have spent the most time in school. They acquire great detailed information and Patton believes that these are the people who are most in need of Soul. He uses the word "personality," but as we have seen he uses this word interchangeably with Soul.

Patton believes, quite correctly, that the ability to acquire knowledge in no way gives that person the ability to apply that knowledge. Whether we gain knowledge from military institutions like West Point or business schools like Harvard, academic excellence is not the secret to victory. We all know articulate idiots who possess reams of knowledge but lack any faculty for its practical application. Patton had little patience for these people.

When the prying spade of the unbiased investigator has removed the muck...from the swamp of the World War, then the skeletons of many such military mammoths will be discovered. Amidst their mighty remains will lurk elusive the secret of German failure.

Beyond question, no soldiers ever sought more diligently for pre-war perfection. *They built and tested and adjusted*

their mighty machine and became so engrossed in its visible perfection, their masterpiece proved inefficient through lack of the divine afflatus, the Soul of a leader.

Patton believed that there was no war machine quite like the German machine prior to WWI. How could they be defeated? No amount of technical genius will substitute for Soul on the battlefield supplied by an inspired leader. No corporation with technical wizardry can lead to sustained success without inspired leadership infusing the enterprise with "divine afflatus," which means inspiration. Soul lies outside the realm of visible perfection, and therefore victory and success also lie beyond this realm.

Here we must most vigorously deny that anything in our remarks is intended to imply belief in the existence of spontaneous, untutored inspiration. With the single exception of the divinely inspired Joan of Arc, no such phenomenon has ever existed...*We must require and must demand all possible thoughtful preparation, and studious effort possible*, so that in war our officers may be equal to their mighty trust--the safety of our country.

Our purpose is not to discourage such preparation simply to call attention to certain defects in its pursuit. **To direct it not towards the glorification of the means--study, but the end--victory.**

Patton believes that divine inspiration, or Soul, favors the prepared mind. He does not want to be misunderstood to sound as if he is against scholarship. Learning one's trade is essential to success. He is not a dualistic thinker that believes in one side of the dichotomy to the peril of the other. His audience was to a group (fellow officers) who believed in the infallibility of reason--much like many of today's corporate CEOs and managers. So with his audience in mind, he continues to stress the limits of reason. He wants to direct the pursuit of knowledge toward the only purpose he has in mind--the end victory.

We must guard against becoming so engrossed in the specific nature of the roots and bark of the trees of knowledge as to miss the meaning and grandeur of the forest they compose.

Our means of studying war have increased as much as our tools for waging it, but it is an open question as to whether this increase in means has not perhaps obscured or obliterated one essential detail, namely *the necessity for personal leadership...*

All down the immortal line of mighty warriors the same is true. Hannibal, Caesar, Heraclius, Charlemagne, Richard, Gustavus, Turenne, Frederick, Napoleon, Grant, Lee, Hindenburg, Allenby, Foch, and Pershing, were all deeply imbued with the *whole knowledge of war* as practiced at their several epochs.

Whether seeking to understand war or corporate affairs, we cannot surrender to a view of reality that reduces what we are looking at to such minute details that we lose sight of the larger picture--the totality that represents the "grandeur of the forest." The whole knowledge of war is necessary, but not enough.

But also, and mark this, so were many of their defeated opponents. *As has been pointed out, the secret of victory lies not wholly in knowledge. It lurks invisible in the vitalizing spark, intangible, yet as evident in the lightning--the warrior Soul.*

There is no better illustration of the potency of this vitalizing element than is portrayed in the story of the "Maid of Orleans" [Joan of Arc]. For more than 90 years prior to her advent, the armies of France had suffered almost continuous defeat at the hands of their British opponents. The reason for this state of things lay not in the inferiority of French valor, but in the reappearance of the foot soldier armed with the missile weapon--the longbow--as the temporary dominating influence on the battlefield. As a result of the recurrence of this tactical condition, France suffered almost continuous defeats with the result that her people lost confidence. They developed an inferiority complex.

Then came Joan, whose flaming faith in her heaven-sent mission rekindled the national spirit. Yet, as great as were her powers, it is idle to suppose that, all unschooled in war as she was, she could have directed, unaided, the energy that was produced. Like the fire beneath the broiler, she produced the steam...

Patton is saying that the passion and energy emanating from Soul needs direction. What can guide this enormous power? Reason supplied by those who lack inspiration may possess enough faculties to direct even heaven sent passion and energy. Patton clearly believes that a leader is supposed to supply the passion, energy, and Soul to an organization. This is another secret to victory.

The happy coincidence of her ignorant enthusiasm and their uninspired intelligence produced the phenomenal series of victories which freed France.

It seems a far cry from the Virgin Maiden to the professional pugilist, yet there is much in the way of their simi-

larity in their dominant characteristics. *In all closely contested ring battles between opponents of equal weight, the decision almost invariably goes to the fighter who is better endowed with faith, self-confidence, and a courageous spirit. But, we must again point out that no pugilist, no matter how confident or courageous, has ever succeeded over an enemy unless to his special attributes he has added the combined knowledge of, and skill at, his profession.*

"Ignorant enthusiasm," which is passion without reason can team up with "uninspired intelligence," which is reason without passion. Success cannot be sustained without both. One must learn about one's profession, whatever it is, be it pugilist, warrior, or CEO. But also skill without Soul is inert material. If we cannot overcome the duality of Soul and reason within ourselves, a valid course of action is to ally yourself with the other half of the duality. If this combination conquered France, it should work for capturing a market!

Patton wants to reemphasize that no amount of inspiration can lead to victory without adding the combined knowledge and skill to the mix. Whatever your profession, there is no shortcut to victory or success that bypasses preparation.

We shall now seek to evaluate and place in their just ratio the three essentials to victory; Inspiration, Knowledge, and Force (Mass).

Considering Napoleon as the apogee of military ability, we note that whereas he won many battles with numbers inferior to the enemy, he never lost a battle when he was numerically superior. In other words, even his transcendent ability was not equal, on every occasion, to the task of counterbalancing numerical inferiority...

So it was with Caesar. Against the Nervae he was a consuming flame, yet against Romans a successful contender. Grant in the Wilderness was as nothing compared to Grant at Donaldson before Vicksburg.

The three preceding cases represent the highest type both mentally and spiritually, but perhaps a shade more emphasis on the spiritual side.

By way of contrast we may note how the learned, but uninspired, Prussians of 1870 triumphed over the poorly led French while, in 1914, their equally uninspired descendents were far less successful in the face of better opposition.

We may therefore postulate that no one element, be it Soul, Knowledge, or Mass is dominant; that a combination of any two of these factors gives a strong presumption of success over an adversary relying on one alone, and that the three combined are practically invincible against a combination of any other two.

Patton identifies the three essentials of success; Soul, which he uses interchangeably with many words including inspiration, Knowledge (reason), and Force (mass). We have spoken about Soul and reason, but what is this force-mass thing? My first reading suggested that Patton was in some way alluding to the equivalence of mass and energy. But Patton, though educated, was not schooled in the physics of his day. He was referring instead to the resources at a leader's disposal. In war that would be armaments, gas, troops, etc. To the corporation, force would refer to capital and personnel.

He attempts to apply a ratio as to "how much" Soul, Knowledge, or Force is required for victory. While admirable, this is not possible and he misses the mark. We cannot quantify Soul. But he *does* identify the likelihood of success if these three essentials are forged together. His methodology may be weak but his insight brilliant. Below he compares the state of US prospects for success against that of others. All CEOs need to do a proper analysis of the competition as well.

Comparing our own resources as to mass with those of any other possible opponent or group of opponents, we strike at least a balance.

The demonstrated ability of our trained leaders in the past wars show that, so far as education is concerned, our officers have no superiors and few equals. This being so, victory will fly to or desert our standards in exact proportion to the presence, or absence, in our leaders of the third attribute [Soul]. Of what does it consist?

U.S. resources and knowledgeable commanders were at least comparable to their counterparts. Patton squarely believes the decisive characteristic of victory lay in the development of Inspiration, Passion, Intuition, Creativity--those reflected attributes of Soul.

As has been noted, the records of all trades and professions show that it is the rare individual, rising like a mountain peak through the clouds of billowing mediocrity, who attains success.

He starts from the same upper reaches, be it hill or hero; yet the cataclysm which causes the former is imponderable as the conditions which produce the latter. So it seems...so surely is the leader the product of obscure, yet ascertainable, circumstances.

The future happiness and existence of races cannot be relegated to the realm of uncertainty contained in the plausible but indefinite assurance that, 'Genius is born, not made.'...Certainly, despite a superabundance of educated aspirants [in WWI], none of the participants produced an inspired leader.

It would be impious to attribute this dearth to God alone. The system of military education, and be it noted, the universal system (of the draft) must be at fault.

Patton does believe that genius can both be made and born. The old Nature/Nurture debate is not being taken up as an either/or situation. He overcomes this dichotomy by acknowledging Nature's role then sets about to tackle the inadequate attempts at education of our leaders. His reasoning still holds true when it comes to educating our business leaders.

...'As a man thinketh, so is he'...contain[s] an infinity of truth. Dry knowledge, like dry rot, destroys the soundest fiber. *A constant search for Soulless fundamentals*, the efforts to regularize the irregular, to make complex the simple, to assume perfect men, perfect material, and perfect terrain as the prerequisites to war, has the same effect on the soldier student...

What a wondrously poetic way of saying that we can destroy our brightest students, our soundest fiber, by pursuing professional education without the fundamentals of Soul. In our military and economic educational institutions we spend much time on technical issues but little time on Soul. Patton is not an evangelist and he is not talking about religion. He is writing about searching and teaching about Soulful fundamentals that are secular, yet spiritual.

War is conflict. Fighting is an elemental exposition of the age-old effort to survive. It is the cold glitter of the attacker's eye, not the point of the questing bayonet, that breaks the line. It is the fierce determination of the driver to close with the enemy, not the mechanical perfection of the tank, that conquers the trench. It is the cataclysmic ecstasy of conflict in the flier, not the perfection of his machine gun, which drops the enemy in flaming ruin. *Yet, volumes are devoted to armaments; and only pages to inspiration...*

How true this is! Recalling my own business education, few pages were devoted to inspiration, values, responsibility, passion, and the essence of greatness. These less formal topics have a place in the classroom and boardroom. If one, as a leader, could spark the "cataclysmic ecstasy of conflict" in a WWI pilot, if one could foster and inspire the creative impulse of a computer programmer, lift the passion and energy level of a sales force, or develop a vision for your department or company utilizing the many faceted gifts of Soul, then you will distinguish yourself. You will poke your head above the clouds of mediocrity.

Obsessed with admiration for the intelligence which history has ascribed to past leaders, *he forgets the inseparable connection between plans, the fruit of the intellect, and execution, the fruit of the Soul...***Hugging the notion of 'intelligence,' he pictures armies of insensate pawns moving with precision of machines...**

Doubtless, he further assumes this same superhuman intelligence will translate those somber sentences into words of fire, which shall electrify his chessmen into frenzied heroes who, heedless of danger, shall dauntlessly translate the stillborn infants of his brain into heroic deeds.

Was it so with Caesar as he rallied the 12th Legion? Could the trackless ether have conveyed to his soldiers via the medium of radio waves the inspiration that Napoleon imparted by his ubiquitous presence when before Rivoli he rode five horses to death, 'To see everything for himself'?

Staff systems and mechanical communications are valuable, but above and beyond them must be the commander. Not as a disembodied brain linked to his men by lines of wire and radio waves, but as a living presence, an all pervading visible personality.

Patton eloquently pleads for uniting the intellect and Soul. Reason can be substituted for intelligence in his writings. He does not want our reason to dehumanize our troops into insensate pawns. It is interesting to note that a Tibetan Monk thinks executing simple tasks like washing dishes can be a Soulful experience and yet we treat even our most momentous activities as if Soul were nonexistent. Patton believes executing plans must be Soulful if success is to be gained. This is not achieved by treating soldiers or workers as if they were machines devoid of feelings.

A leader must convey passion to the troops. Napoleon rode five horses to death! Patton was always near the front lines and showed himself to the troops in WWII. He took his own advice. If you run a department or company and you do not show yourself to the "troops," how can your passion be conveyed? By memo? By telephone? E-mail? Nothing replaces the connection between leader and follower face to face.

...[The secret of success lies] **in the inspiring spirit with which** [commanders] **so inoculated their soldiers as to lift** weary footsore men out of themselves and to make them march, forgetful of agony, as did Massena's division after Rivoli or Jackson's at Winchester...

The ability to produce endurance is but an instance of that same martial Soul which arouses in its followers that resistless emotion defined as élan...It is akin to that almost cataleptic burst of physical and mental exuberance shown by the athlete when he breaks a record or plunges through the tacklers, and by the author or artist in the creation of a masterpiece. The difference is that in the athlete or artist, the ebullition is auto-stimulated. With an army, it is the result of external impetus--leadership.

When you build an organization or department, it is up to the leader to infuse the enterprise with that vital spirit. When your people are weary, you must arouse them. You must supply them with energy. I depart from Patton when he suggests that athletes supply their own energy. In team sports this can be achieved from the roar of the crowd or an inspiring talk from a Lombardi or Riley. But it is the case that good leaders bring passion to their profession.

In considering war, we must avoid that adoration of the *material as exemplified by scientists who deny the existence of aught they cannot cut or weigh*...History as read does not divulge the source of leadership. Hence, its study often induces us to forget its potency.

As a mirror shows us not ourselves, but our reflection, so it is with Soul and with leadership. We know them but by the acts they inspire or results they have achieved.

Here is Patton's simple statement against philosophical materialism. He does not want to reduce reality to things you can cut or weigh. There are other things that exist beyond that which we can measure like Soul.

We get to understand Soul indirectly. Jung called this method "circumnabulation" or talking around a subject to elucidate it. Patton comes close to the Biblical analogy of knowing a tree, "by the fruit it bears." We see the Soul at work by its fruit.

Like begets like. In the armies of the great we seek the reflections of themselves and we find: Self-confidence; Enthusiasm; Abnegation of the self; Loyalty; and Courage.

Resolution, no matter how so adamant, mated to knowledge, no matter how so infinite, never begat such a progeny.

Such offspring arises only from blood lines as elemental as themselves. The leader must be incarnate of them...

When like begets like, Patton is suggesting that we reap what we sow. If we have dignity, honor, passion, and Soul, then we will receive this type of effort from those around us.

We see reflections of the Soul in the traits great leaders have exhibited. Resolving to acquire these traits does not insure their acquisition. Even when that resolution is wedded to "infinite knowledge," there is no progeny without Soul. Only when these traits emanate from the Soul does the leader emerge from its expression.

There are certainly born leaders, but *the soldier may still overcome his natal defects by unremitting effort and prac-*

tice...The enthusiasm which permits the toil and promises the achievement is simply an all-absorbing preoccupation in the profession elected.

Loyalty is frequently only considered as faithfulness from the bottom up. It has another and equally important application; that is from the top down. *One of the most frequently noted characteristics of the great (who remained great) is unforgetfulness of and loyalty to their subordinates.* It is this characteristic which binds, with hoops of iron, their juniors to them.

A man who is truly and unselfishly loyal to his superiors is of necessity so to his juniors, and they to him.

Courage, moral and physical, is almost a synonym of all the foregoing traits. It fosters the resolution to combat and cherishes the ability to assume responsibility, be it for successes or for failures.

Can a man then acquire these characteristics? The answer is: they *have*--they can. For, 'As a man thinketh, so is he.'

The fixed determination to acquire the warrior Soul, and have acquired it to either conquer or perish with honor, is the *Secret of Victory*.

--Maj. George S. Patton Jr.
March 26, 1926

Patton does not want to give the impression that we cannot overcome "natal defects." Through perseverance of spirit and study, a leader can become great. He must be selfless toward his men and courageous in assuming responsibility. How often have you seen managers run for cover to avoid responsibility? It is all too common. Its practice can never lead to greatness.

Patton comes full circle and gives hope to those not born with all the natural gifts from the Creator: "As a man thinketh, so is he." This combined with the journey to acquire not only knowledge but the **Warrior Soul** is the path to victory. This journey is a sacred journey for every profession. Those who instinctively understand this are given a gift from above. Those who come to understand that this Soulful journey itself is what makes greatness prevail.

Epilogue

"...our large social institutions subscribe to the concepts and values of an outdated world-view, to a paradigm that is inadequate for dealing with problems of our overpopulated, globally-interconnected world. At the same time, researchers at the leading edge of science [and] various social movements are developing a new vision of reality that will form the basis of our future technologies, economic systems, and social institutions."

--Fritjof Capra, *The Tao Of Physics*

So now we have come full circle regarding Corporate Soul. We are no closer to defining what exactly Soul is than when we first started the journey. It has been suggested that this book's target may be too exclusionary. Since the topic of a soulful life is of interest to each and every one of us, why limit the audience by applying a "Corporate" header?

To this charge I have no answer except to say that this might be true. While I have the utmost respect for science, art, philosophy and literature, I am first and foremost a student and practitioner of business. My growth as an entrepreneur and executive has mirrored a personal spiritual growth.

What I have tried to do is make soulful discourse relevant to an audience that has one of the largest influences in our everyday lives and attempt to develop a new vision of reality. To encourage this discourse in corporate boardrooms and managerial departments is not only humane, but makes business sense, too.

What will the face of tomorrow's corporation look like? Will the face be accompanied by a spirit and heart that believes in the value of recognizing Soul? Will we begin to have our leaders take responsibility for bringing Soul into the workplace?

To infuse one's vision with Soul is not just a "nice idea;" it is necessary! Why? If we want our vision accepted and embraced enthusiastically, then having Soul reflected in that vision helps draw others toward its adoption. The fusion of vision with Soul in a sense creates a harmony that resonates throughout an organization, city, country, and even the Universe.

By infusing our corporations with passion and energy, we acknowledge our responsibility to fellow workers and give instead of take. The giving itself not only nourishes others but ourselves as well.

Once we discover the interconnection of which Chief Seattle spoke, that whatever we do to the web of life we do to ourselves, then new ways of accepting responsibility assumes its rightful place in corporate America.

By tapping into the qualities of Soul, we in some ways tap into the infinite. By understanding that we are connected with each other and linked with the air, trees, and even the stars, we are empowered. By releasing our ego-defined world, we are free to unite with absolutely everything else. This is the true beauty and wonder of Soul.

Corporations do not really exist except as lifeless fictions that simulate life. They are composed of real-life human beings who too often reflect the lifeless fictions that employ them. Developing Corporate Soul is about making our fictions reflect our humanity and values. It is up to us to breathe the life force of Soul into our institutions.

To do this, we must release the vestigial qualities of Soul that we all possess. We must rediscover today what was once the most natural state of affairs before reason became our only guiding principle. The unforgiving, knife-like edge of reason and rationality has carved Soul from our everyday lives. This in turn has created institutions from the family to corporations with the same disregard for Soul.

We must remember that we create our fictions. Like dreams, they reflect our perceptions and internal realities. They then, in turn, impact our lives in almost a cosmic harmony of dancing partners who take turns at the lead. Searching for Soul and allowing it to enter into our lives will transform our fictions and make them reflect our humanity.

In doing this, it is not the case that we need to "feel more and think less." We must not surrender to the polar opposite of reason. We tried this in the Middle Ages resulting in superstition, Inquisitions, and magic carrying the day. We need to transcend the duality between thinking and feeling.

The synthesis allows for the flowering of human potential. Realizing human potential requires constant diligence and energy. The creative tension between reason and feeling is itself one of the sources of energy. Certainly it is one of the wondrous aspects of being human.

In the end, we must always remind ourselves that it is within our power to change the world, corporation, and our individual Self. We must first decide. In the words of one of the greatest philosophers/poets, Goethe:

> "The moment one definitely commits oneself, then providence moves, too. All sorts of things occur to help one that would never otherwise have occurred. A whole stream of events issues from the decision, raising in one's favor all manner of unforeseen incidents and meetings and material assistance which no man could have dreamed would have come his way. Whatever you can do or dream you can, begin it. Boldness has genius, power and magic in it. Begin it now."